A GIFT FOR:

_____

FROM:

_____

DATE:

_____

MIDNIGHT
DAD
Devotional

100 *Devotions* AND *Prayers*
TO CONNECT DADS JUST LIKE YOU TO THE FATHER

BECKY THOMPSON
AND DR. MARK PITTS

THOMAS NELSON
Since 1798

Midnight Dad Devotional

© 2021 Mark R. Pitts and Rebecca F. Thompson

Cover Art Copyright © 2020 Raahat Kaduji

Published in Nashville, Tennessee, by Thomas Nelson. Thomas Nelson is a registered trademark of HarperCollins Christian Publishing, Inc.

Front cover illustrated by Raahat Kaduji.

Thomas Nelson titles may be purchased in bulk for educational, business, fund-raising, or sales promotional use. For information, please email SpecialMarkets@ThomasNelson.com.

ISBN 978-1-4002-2833-1 (HC)
ISBN 978-1-4002-2835-5 (eBook)
ISBN 978-1-4002-2832-4 (audiobook)

Printed in the United States of America

21 22 23 24 25 LakeBook 10 9 8 7 6 5 4 3 2 1

For my wife, Susan, who has been my best friend for more than forty years. Thank you for your encouragement and support throughout the creation of this book.

For my daughter, Becky, who reminds me every day that I don't have to be afraid to chase a dream. Thank you for showing me the way to get where I was going.
MARK

For my dad, Mark Pitts, who has lived out the message of this book. I learned the Father's love through yours.

"Here's our . . ."
BECKY

CONTENTS

INTRODUCTION

To you, Dad, before we begin . . .

I'm not sure how this book came to be in your possession. I'm not sure what you were looking for or what someone you love was thinking when this book was purchased. What I do know is what you'll find inside.

Our prayer is that each of these one hundred devotions connects you to the heart, wisdom, and strength of your Father in heaven. That's the mission we've been assigned.

Who are we? I am Dr. Mark Pitts, Becky Thompson's dad. We cowrote this book together. I met and married my wife, Susan, while I was attending the University of Tulsa College of Law, where I earned a Juris Doctorate degree. I have two grown daughters, Beth and Becky (of course). Together, we have been in part-time or full-time ministry for thirty-eight years, establishing and planting churches and starting dozens of new ministries.

A few years ago, Becky began a nightly prayer ministry online called Midnight Mom Devotional, reaching out to moms all across the world. Soon, she invited Susan to help her lead this ministry. Each night, with a short devotion and prayer, they connected women to each other and to the hope of Jesus.

Not surprisingly, as a family we began to feel as though the mission of this ministry was expanding to create a space to reach dads as well. And so the Midnight Dad Devotional was created long before you held this book in your hands. We've been praying for dads just like you for years now in our online community.

However, I didn't want to limit this work to just a set of nightly prayers. Instead, I wanted to give dads an opportunity to see themselves in the words of Scripture. I wanted them to understand that, with the exception of Jesus, God has always used ordinary people to do remarkable things.

That's where you come in, Dad. You are a man God can use. God knows we are imperfect. And the sooner we dads recognize that fact, the sooner we can exchange those imperfections for His goodness. And isn't that what you really want? To be more like Him and still rest in His peace, His security, and His blessing?

I want you to see yourself in these biblical examples and believe that you have (or can have) God's love safely and securely in your heart. At the same time, I don't want you to settle. I hope you realize there is always a better or a best to the good you already are.

God has called you to the role of father, and you have God Himself as a role model. All these devotions and prayers are intended to draw you closer to God's heart. He is, of course, the perfect Father, and He wants you to come up higher and closer to His standard. The examples in this book are intended to show you that you are already on that journey, and you can make it.

We are praying for you as you begin.

Dr. Mark Pitts and Becky Thompson

1

TONIGHT WE PRAY FOR THE DAD WHO KNOWS GOD AS HIS FATHER

$\mathcal{D}$ad, as we embark on our journey of discovering our role as fathers, the most important thing we can understand is that we, ourselves, have a heavenly Father who loves us, cares for us, and provides for us, just as we love, care for, and provide for our children. By understanding God as Father, we understand who we are as dads. Jesus taught us about knowing our Father.

Matthew 6:9 says, "This, then, is how you should pray: 'Our Father in heaven, hallowed be your name'" (NIV). Take notice. Jesus didn't say "My Father." He didn't say, "Oh, God, Creator of the universe." He said to His disciples (and to us) to pray to God as though we have a personal relationship with Him.

At the time these words were spoken, this was a seismic shift in the people's understanding of God. This was the first time in Scripture anyone had been taught to pray to God as their own Father. The people could only understand that God was God. Jesus expanded the peoples' hearts to believe exactly who God could be to them: a Dad.

The same may be true for us. We have been taught that God is God, but we forget He is our Father. So, Dad, a note right here at the beginning: you have a Father. In every circumstance, every trial, He is waiting to hear from you. He wants to hear your heart. As you go through these devotions, daily, weekly, or however often you enter in, remember that you can look to Him, your Dad, to carry you through whatever you are facing. He wants every good thing for you just as you want every good thing for your children. And more than anything, He wants to connect with your heart.

LET'S PRAY

Lord, as this dad prays to You in the words that Jesus taught us to pray, "Our Father in heaven," help him understand the true meaning of that relationship. Help him to know the joy and the power and the goodness of that relationship. As You reveal Yourself in these next ninety-nine teachings, help him capture what is in Your heart so he can be the best dad for his children by better knowing You as his Father. In Jesus' name we pray. Amen.

CONTINUE THE CONNECTION

Take a moment to pray the Lord's Prayer.
It is found in Matthew 6:9–13.

2

TONIGHT WE PRAY FOR THE DAD WHO HAS QUESTIONS

*I*t's okay to have questions about the things Jesus taught and said and did. After all, the events in the Gospels took place about two thousand years ago. There were different customs, different cultures, and different ways to look at the world. Sometimes, as a modern man, it can be difficult to understand everything that was happening. It was okay then, and it's okay now to ask questions.

There was one such man in Scripture named Nicodemus who had many questions. He was a renowned teacher in Israel who believed that God had said everything that needed to be said in the Old Testament writings. He lived his life teaching this concept. For most of his life, he was certain he was correct. Until Jesus of Nazareth came.

The Scripture says, "Now there was a Pharisee, a man named Nicodemus who was a member of the Jewish ruling council. He came to Jesus at night and said, 'Rabbi, we know that you are a teacher who has come from God. For no one could perform the signs you are doing if God were not with him'" (John 3:1–2 NIV).

Nicodemus wanted to know from Jesus just how He came from God. They had a lengthy conversation, which included the famous words, "For God so loved the world that he gave his one and only Son, that whoever believes in him shall not perish but have eternal life" (v. 16 NIV). Nicodemus asked his questions and Jesus gave His answers. There is no other recorded contact between them.

Listen, Dad—while it is okay to ask questions, what you do with the answers is even more important. When you receive your answers, allow them to bring you closer to the Lord. Allow your story to be richer and deeper. Allow the answers to change your life as well.

LET'S PRAY

Lord, sometimes this dad has questions, and he wants answers. He believes that only You have the real answers to the questions in his life. Just as any good father stands ready to answer the honest questions of his child, so You desire to answer Your children. Show him that You are never out of his reach. In Jesus' name we pray. Amen.

CONTINUE THE CONNECTION

What are you bringing to Jesus this week?

What answers are you listening for?

3

TONIGHT WE PRAY FOR THE DAD WHO IS ALWAYS PREPARED

*W*hen you think of the word *prepared*, what comes to mind? You probably think about having the right equipment or knowledge or attitude. Preparation looks different for each of us, but I'd define it this way: preparation is the soul of success.

When it comes to being a dad, you have prepared all of your life for the opportunity to lead, guide, and direct a family. It's your responsibility. You know it. Whether or not you were raised in a home where your dad prepared every day to make a way for his family, you feel the weight of it for yours. You want to be able to say that with Christ's help you've done your best in all circumstances that day. That you've left nothing out. That when the lights are out, and it's quiet, and just before you fall asleep, you know that this day, and everything else associated with it, is complete. Isn't that what you really want? That's why you prepare.

Scripture reminds us in Proverbs 16:9, "A man's heart plans his way, but the LORD directs his steps" (NKJV). We must understand here that it is the Lord who provides the goal, sets the vision, and determines the outcome. While we can and should make our plans, no plans should be made without our heavenly Father's influence. So also, while we do our part to prepare our lives, we cannot overlook the importance of looking to God to prepare our hearts and minds. He knows what's up ahead. We bring our best offering. He takes the desires of our hearts and wraps them in wisdom and grace. Together we can face anything.

LET'S PRAY

Lord, this dad has learned that the better he prepares for each day, the easier that day progresses, the more he achieves, and the more successful he feels. He looks to You to prepare His heart and mind. Give this dad who has already prepared for tomorrow a good night's sleep with the peace he richly deserves. In Jesus' name we pray. Amen.

CONTINUE THE CONNECTION

As you pray this week, what is it that you are preparing for that you need God's help with in order to succeed? He is more than willing to meet you at the place of your need and walk you through it.

4

TONIGHT WE PRAY FOR THE DAD WHO IS WISE

*I*n Matthew 7:24–27, Jesus shared a story of two homes:

> Everyone who hears these words of mine and puts them into prac-
> tice is like a wise man who built his house on the rock. The rain
> came down, the streams rose, and the winds blew and beat against
> that house; yet it did not fall, because it had its foundation on the
> rock. But everyone who hears these words of mine and does not put
> them into practice is like a foolish man who built his house on sand.
> The rain came down, the streams rose, and the winds blew and beat
> against that house, and it fell with a great crash. (NIV)

You have likely heard this story before. It's an obvious analogy
that is easy for us to apply to our lives. We build our families on the
hope of Jesus as the Rock, and when life's storms come, we are able
to withstand them. Those who heard this story at the time of Jesus'
telling it understood a much deeper meaning.

When Jesus shared these words, building a house on sand was easier, cheaper, and so much quicker. A house constructed on sand could

be built all at once. But this house was always in danger of collapse. A house built on a rock required much more planning, and because of the additional costs it could often be built only in stages.

As wise dads, we must remember both lessons. We must choose to build our lives on Jesus and His Word, but we must also remember that we choose to build this life day by day, season by season, segment by segment. This is the lifestyle of a wise dad. Daily we choose small, solid victories rather than an easy out, knowing that when we do, we won't have to fear collapse.

LET'S PRAY

Lord, You know that this dad wants to protect his children, and this requires wise choices to move forward. Help him be careful to weigh the risks and take small steps if necessary rather than losing a lot. Your plans are safe, and this dad's family has peace because they know You have provided exactly what they need in every season to build for this moment. Bless this wise dad. In Jesus' name we pray. Amen.

CONTINUE THE CONNECTION

As you pray this week, think about the small victories that have led up to large successes in your life. What were some of them?

5

TONIGHT WE PRAY FOR THE DAD
WHO NEEDS A MIRACLE

As a dad, you have moments when you realize your own limits. At every age your children meet you with new challenges. You press as hard or go as far as you can, and yet it doesn't seem to be enough. Further effort is required, yet you have reached your limit. You need a miracle. You need something only God can do. One dad in Scripture named Jairus experienced just this.

In Jesus' day, religious leaders were credited with certain medical knowledge and expertise. They were not healers, but they could recommend certain therapies that were effective. But Jairus's daughter was sick, and Jairus had done all there was to do for her. Can you imagine his desperation? If you were one of those religious leaders and neither you nor anyone you knew had the expertise to heal your child? Now imagine your last gasp of hope lived in the person of a relatively unknown healer named Jesus of Nazareth, someone rumored to be performing miracles. What would you do? You'd likely do what we all would. Whatever it takes. Jairus did just that. He went to Jesus, knowing he had reached his own limit. And Mark 5:35–36 records, "While He was still speaking, people came from the synagogue leader's house and said, 'Your daughter is dead. Why bother the Teacher anymore?' But when Jesus overheard what was said, He told the synagogue leader, 'Don't be afraid. Only believe.'" Jairus listened to Jesus, and at the end of the day, his daughter was completely healed.

As a dad you try to find help for your children. You won't let anything get in between you and them. You will put aside everything that stands between your own life and theirs. You will fight to your last breath to see them whole. Jesus reminded Jairus that fear would not heal his child. But believing in the saving power of Jesus would. Jairus did, and so can you. Today let's believe for a miracle in your life and for your family!

LET'S PRAY

Lord, Jairus planned for success. Yet ultimately he needed Your power. This dad is willing to look to You for Your answers because he believes You honor Your promises. Continue to give him confidence to always bring his needs to You in prayer in every circumstance, no matter how desperate. In Jesus' name we pray. Amen.

CONTINUE THE CONNECTION

This week as you pray, remember those who are desperate for a miracle and include them in your petitions to the Lord.

6

TONIGHT WE PRAY FOR THE DAD WHO KNOWS THAT RAISING CHILDREN IS AN IMPORTANT MISSION

*A*lthough it might not seem on the outside to be an assignment that will change the world, the task God has appointed to us will do just that. We are called to be fathers. Our mission is made up of a million small and yet highly significant moments. Each one matters, even if we don't easily see it.

There is a story in Scripture about men who helped Jesus fulfill His mission. Because Jesus was the Messiah, the One who had been foretold by prophets, it was of the utmost importance that Jesus fulfill every prophetic word spoken about the Messiah in the Old Testament. During the celebration of the Passover week, in which Jesus would be crucified, one of the more obscure events that was foretold declared that the Messiah would enter Jerusalem riding on a donkey. But in order for that scripture to be fulfilled, it was very important that someone go get the donkey.

Mark 11:1–2 records, "When they approached Jerusalem, at Bethphage and Bethany near the Mount of Olives, He sent two of His disciples and told them, 'Go into the village ahead of you. As soon as you enter it, you will find a young donkey tied there, on which no one has ever sat. Untie it and bring it here.'"

Jesus fulfilled the Scriptures at every turn of His life because He was the Messiah, and the Old Testament foretells that fact. Just like this moment with the donkey, some things have to be taken care of at a particular time, for a particular reason, by particular people. Sometimes we just don't see the importance of what we are doing in our roles as dads, but everything you do as a father is important. It might not always seem like it. But destinies are created one mission at a time.

LET'S PRAY

Lord, this dad loves his job as father, and when he awakes, he makes sure he's ready to accomplish his mission. He believes that each day is a gift from God and that he has a responsibility to take care of it. He holds his family close, whether he's physically near or far, and completes the mission God has given him for them. In Jesus' name we pray. Amen.

CONTINUE THE CONNECTION

As you go through your week, pay attention to the little missions, remembering each small moment fulfills a greater call.

7

TONIGHT WE PRAY FOR THE DAD WHO NEEDS FORGIVENESS

*O*n the day Jesus was crucified, two men were led down a road and up a hill with Him to a place of crucifixion. Jesus was nailed to His cross first, followed by the other men in turn, one on either side of Him. During the day, as the crowds came for this very public execution, some of the people watching berated and mocked Jesus, daring Him to save Himself and come down from the cross.

Jesus asked His Father not to hold these injustices against them. Finally, one of the robbers who was being crucified chided Him and told Jesus that He should save Himself and "us," meaning the two crucified with Him. As Luke told the story, it appears that the two robbers knew each other and they were very bad men. Scripture reflects that these were thieves who had shown no remorse for their crimes. It was also clear that only one of the men was penitent.

Luke 23:40–43 records that the second robber rebuked the first, saying,

"Don't you even fear God, since you are undergoing the same punishment? We are punished justly, because we're getting back what we deserve for the things we did, but this man has done nothing wrong." Then he said, "Jesus, remember me when You come into Your kingdom!" And He said to him, "I assure you: Today you will be with Me in paradise."

Jesus knew what was in this man's heart, and when he asked Jesus to remember him, Jesus replied with an assurance that he would experience the presence of God on that very day. This man's heart had been changed, perhaps at the last minute, and Jesus heard his prayer. Jesus forgave the small injustices as well as the large crimes. Dad, He stands ready to forgive you as well.

LET'S PRAY

Lord, this dad may think he is unforgivable. He needs to know that You are a forgiving God and that it is Your desire to be in a relationship with all Your children. He needs to know that there doesn't have to be a perfect time to ask for forgiveness. You are always ready to hear his prayer. Speak to his willing heart when he asks. In Jesus' name we pray. Amen.

CONTINUE THE CONNECTION

Take a moment to reconnect with your heavenly Father by asking for forgiveness. He already knows, but there is a powerful exchange in the asking and receiving.

8

TONIGHT WE PRAY FOR THE DAD WHO JUST BECAME A DAD

*B*ecoming a dad comes upon us in a myriad of circumstances. But, generally speaking, we become dads in a hospital, a home, or a court-room. When you first find out you're going to be a dad, it can be overwhelming. Even if you've planned for it, the actual news can cause you to step back for a second. It doesn't matter where you are in life; the announcement of your fatherhood brings a rush of emotions to all of us. In the Scriptures, Zechariah was one such father who received that news. Except he received it from an angel. Which, in its own right, was an astonishing circumstance. We read his story in Luke 1:18–20:

"How can I know this?" Zechariah asked the angel. "For I am an old man, and my wife is well along in years." The angel answered him, "I am Gabriel, who stands in the presence of God, and I was sent to speak to you and tell you this good news. Now listen! You will become silent and unable to speak until the day these things take place, because you did not believe my words, which will be fulfilled in their proper time."

Zechariah had sought after God continuously throughout his life and ministry. He prayed for the opportunity to show his worthiness as a father and also as a priest. You see, priests were often fathers because of a man's age when he became a priest. Throughout Scripture we see priestly fathers representing the children of Israel to God. Zechariah would now have his own child to present to the Lord. As the angel delivered this news, Zechariah was so surprised that, just for a moment, he wondered if he'd heard correctly.

Dad, God understands that the announcement of being a father can be quite overwhelming. But you can trust that He will be with you every step of the way. You can do this with His help, and it will be one of the most wonderful things in your life.

LET'S PRAY

Lord, help this dad in his wonderful role of fatherhood as he learns to wear the mantle proudly and gladly. Please show him that through Christ he is able to rise to this challenge. Remind him that fatherhood is a joy. Whether this child is his first or one of several, remind him that You continue to walk with him daily and teach him how to be a great dad. In Jesus' name we pray. Amen.

CONTINUE THE CONNECTION

This week as you pray, remember the new dads you know. This may be a difficult season for them, and they will appreciate your prayers and support.

9

TONIGHT WE PRAY FOR THE DAD WHO KNOWS THE IMPORTANCE OF PRAYER

*W*e live in a busy world, don't we? It's easy for prayer to drop down the list of what must be done, but we cannot overlook the importance of it. In the time of Jesus, people prayed at least three times a day, reciting specific prayers. One of these daily prayers can be found in Deuteronomy 6:4: "Listen, Israel: The LORD our God, the LORD is One." In fulfilling all prophecies, Jesus would have prayed this prayer every day as a rabbi.

In Matthew 22:36–37, a lawyer came to Jesus and asked, "'Teacher, which command in the law is the greatest?' He [Jesus] said to him, 'Love the Lord your God with all your heart, with all your soul, and with all your mind.'"

Jesus reminded the lawyer that this instruction to love God was found in the verse immediately following the prayer, a prayer the lawyer prayed every day. That prayer declaring that God is One reflected the majesty of God, the promises of God, and the righteousness of God. He is everything and provides everything we need. Jesus wanted the lawyer to see that a relationship with God was more important than an enumeration of rules and commandments and that we can have a relationship with God when we understand who God is.

So often we need to be reminded of this. We must remember that prayer is so much more than just asking and waiting and hoping. It is a conversation with God that strengthens us to such a degree that we become more like God as we share our hearts with Him. As we do, our hearts are changed into the image of His heart. You see, God wants us to be in relationship with Him even more than we do. The purpose of prayer isn't to reach a certain outcome, but to be transformed by the outpouring of our hearts to God's and His response to us.

LET'S PRAY

Lord, Jesus showed all of us that when we pray we can have a relationship with You, our Father in heaven, the same way He did. This dad wants to see what You see and know what You know. He wants to know Your heart and hear Your words. Help him make prayer the first thing in his life, remembering that every good thing flows from putting You first. In Jesus' name we pray. Amen.

CONTINUE THE CONNECTION

This week do your best to make prayer a priority, whether that means first thing in the morning or as you go throughout your day. Share your heart, trusting there is power in the process.

10

TONIGHT WE PRAY FOR THE DAD WHO USES WHAT'S IN HIS HANDS

*A*s dads, we have a fairly good idea what we're going to encounter in our daily routine. We use tools and provisions in our jobs to accomplish our responsibilities. Those tools are important to us, and we've learned how to use them over time. We are proficient with them. If you are a welder, you use a torch. If you are a carpenter, a hammer and nails are your tools. Your tools might also be a stethoscope or a fire hose. Or even a computer's mouse or your own voice. Whatever the tools are, you use them to provide your family with security and peace.

Moses had spent forty years as a shepherd using his staff. He protected his family by warding off enemies that would steal from them. He used it to protect the sheep, which represented his livelihood, from wolves and bears. He knew this tool and how to use it for a specific purpose. So when God called Moses to return to Egypt to free His people, and Moses wondered how the people would believe that God sent him, God answered in Exodus 4:2, "'What is that in your hand?'

'A staff,' he replied." It was with this staff, once used for sheep, that God performed miracles to bring freedom to His people.

God wanted Moses to know that not only was Moses a man God could use, but also that God could use Moses' own tools to accomplish His plan. He trusted Moses to use what he'd been given to the very best of his ability. And He promised that He would multiply whatever Moses had to achieve God's desired result.

Dad, God knows who you are and your desire to do everything necessary to provide for and protect your children. He's given you exactly the tools you need to take care of them. You may not do something as earth-shattering as parting the Red Sea with your tools. But just like Moses, what you use daily can perform miracles in people's lives when you trust God and use your skills, tools, and talents for His glory.

LET'S PRAY

Lord, we pray for this dad who uses whatever he has available to secure peace for his family. He is dedicated to this role as provider and protector, and he believes he can do that with what he has. Lord, give this dad confidence in his calling, strength in its fulfillment, and the peace that You are responsible for the results. In Jesus' name we pray. Amen.

CONTINUE THE CONNECTION

How can you use the tools in your hands
for God's kingdom this week?

11

TONIGHT WE PRAY FOR THE DAD WHO LEAVES A LEGACY

*W*hen you think of the word *legacy*, what comes to mind? Maybe you think of what you've accomplished in business or your trade. Maybe you think about how years from now, your friends or those in your community will speak about how you served them today. But I wonder if you have ever considered your spiritual legacy.

In Acts 10:1–2 we learn about a man named Cornelius in Caesarea, "a centurion of what was called the Italian Regiment. He was a devout man and feared God along with his whole household. He did many charitable deeds for the Jewish people and always prayed to God." This man was not Jewish, yet he knew God and was considered devout, doing good works for those around him. All the people in the region knew of his reputation for his acts of kindness, which he did without expecting anything in return. Cornelius was a good man, known and respected by many.

Perhaps it was because of his God-fearing heart and reputation for generosity that God decided to use him to shift the course of the apostle Peter's ministry. Peter, the friend and follower of Jesus, spread the good news of the Messiah after Jesus returned to heaven. But Peter's ministry had been to share this news with Jewish men. It wasn't until God sent Peter to meet Cornelius, a non-Jew, that Peter learned something that would change history. When Peter shared about Jesus, all of Cornelius's family was saved. This was wonderful for them and great for us, because it was through their redemption we learned salvation is available for everyone.

Cornelius's kindness left a legacy of character, but his devotion to God left a legacy that affected generations, including us today. What you do for God matters. It matters for you, and it matters for your kids. Don't overlook the importance of your spiritual legacy.

LET'S PRAY

Lord, this dad wants to leave a legacy for his children. He is seeing them change daily. He knows he has to keep up if he's going to have an influence in their lives. He has to show his children that they are loved. As this dad shows the love that You show him, he's beginning his legacy right now. Enlarge his heart to contain more of Your truth and love. In Jesus' name we pray. Amen.

CONTINUE THE CONNECTION

Consider how you are investing today in your children's spiritual inheritance.

12

TONIGHT WE PRAY FOR THE DAD WHO STANDS UP FOR WHAT IS GOOD

Children like to think of their dad as a superhero, especially when they are little. Even the youngest children somehow understand the battle between good and evil, and they think their dad is the person who can set the world straight when evil tries to win. It's why they call out for us when they are scared or alone or need help. It's because they know we stand on the side of love and safety. And we know that we have a God we can look to in the same way.

There is a story in the Bible about a man named Elijah. He was a prophet of God who stood up for the Lord against one of the evilest kings of Israel, Ahab. There came a showdown between Elijah and the evil prophets of Baal set in place by Ahab. The false prophets built an altar and Elijah built an altar. Both called down fire on their sacrifices, but only the true God's fire consumed Elijah's altar.

First Kings 18:39 records, "When all the people saw it, they fell facedown and said, 'Yahweh, He is God! Yahweh, He is God!'" The people responded this way for two reasons. They saw the power of

God. But they saw this power because just before calling down the fire, Elijah had told the people to stand near him. He believed in the goodness of the Lord, and he wanted to show them that God did not and would not fail.

As dads, we stand up for what is good, and we look to the Lord to back us. We believe God will be on our side. We believe He won't fail us. And so we draw our children close to watch. We make sure they have opportunities to see God be big in our circumstances. We make sure they see His power on display.

LET'S PRAY

Lord, this dad isn't here by chance. You placed him in this very important position of showing his children Your truth, righteousness, and goodness. He stands in Your favor and power. Strengthen his resolve to always be ready to take this responsibility. Help him find moments to pull his children close so they see when we align ourselves with what You call good, we have the power to face anything. In Jesus' name we pray. Amen.

CONTINUE THE CONNECTION

This week ask the Lord to help you stand on the side of good, trusting He will stand with you.

13

TONIGHT WE PRAY FOR THE DAD WHO IS SEPARATED FROM HIS KIDS BY DIVORCE

*D*ivorce is a difficult choice to make for a family. God designed marriage to last a lifetime. When a divorce happens, it is painful because it isn't just affecting daily circumstances; it represents a separation of soul from soul and spirit from spirit in a family. God fully recognizes what you have experienced, and He has hope and healing for you and your family. He weeps over divorce in the same way as He weeps over the prospect of being separated from His children. In the kingdom of God, relationships are eternal. Only here on earth can they be made temporal.

Dad, even though you are separated in time, you are never separated in prayer from your children. The ancient Hebrew prayer found in Numbers 6:24–26 is considered a blessing over children. It says, "May Yahweh bless you and protect you; may Yahweh make His face shine on you and be gracious to you; may Yahweh look with favor on you and give you peace."

A Hebrew father always wanted his children to know that God

would provide for their well-being and safety. He wanted them to know that God would hear their prayers, and finally, he wanted them to know that they could trust God in all things. May you always understand that God is in the process of providing for your well-being and safety. God has turned His face toward you to hear what you might request or have need of, and He is predisposed to provide you with what you need.

For generations, this prayer was recited during the Friday evening meal, called Shabbat. The father would pray this over his children weekly. No matter how far in space they were separated, they always had the last Shabbat blessing to carry them through. Dad, we can continue this ancient tradition and pray this scripture over our children, even if they are not with us. There is no distance in prayer.

LET'S PRAY

Lord, we pray for this dad who misses his kids due to a divorce or separation. It breaks his heart when he is not with them. He cares deeply. And his children understand that due to the circumstances he can't always be there, but he does try his best. Lord, make his dedication count. In Jesus' name we pray. Amen.

CONTINUE THE CONNECTION

Pause to pray Numbers 6:24–26 over your children.

14

TONIGHT WE PRAY FOR THE DAD WHO BUILDS FOR HIS FAMILY

*W*e have many responsibilities as dads, but we can never overlook the role of builder. Some of us build cars, some of us build buildings, still others of us build careers. It's part of our nature to build. Very few of us wish to live our lives without a result or something we can aspire to. No matter what you are building, know this: dads have been building for their families' futures since the beginning of time.

Many are familiar with the story of Noah and his family, who built an ark. With this story, we think of the rain. We think of the animals. We think of the rainbow. But this story is actually about a father who partnered with God to build for his family.

Before the doors were closed, only eight persons entered the ark. Genesis 7:13 says, "On that same day Noah along with his sons Shem, Ham, and Japheth, Noah's wife, and his three sons' wives entered the ark with him." God often asks us to accomplish great tasks, and sometimes it is a struggle to come up to it, so to speak. But He always expects that we will include our families in the construction. Some say that it took Noah seventy-five years to build the ark for the animals and eight people. Probably none of us has endeavored more than a normal lifetime to achieve a goal so lofty, yet each of us gives our entire life to build for our family and the generations that will be affected because we did.

You may not be building an actual ark, but you know that everything you do affects your family's future. Some days it's easy and some days it's hard, but it's important to remember that yesterday's effort does not guarantee tomorrow's success. So just keep building.

LET'S PRAY

Lord, this dad knows that he has to be careful with his words and actions to build up and not tear down, because his children's souls are precious. Give this dad Your patience to always stay the course. He has all the necessary tools already in his hands, and You have given him a strategy. Help him see the vision for what You are building in his family's life. In Jesus' name we pray. Amen.

CONTINUE THE CONNECTION

This week as you continue to build for your family, remember that just as the Lord gave Noah directions on how to build the ark, He will give you direction on your efforts as well.

15

TONIGHT WE PRAY FOR THE DAD WHO HAS SINNED

*G*od has always had a plan for you, Dad. That plan involves you and His Son, Jesus Christ. You see, God loves you. And He loves His Son. And He sent His Son to us, to you, so you could know Him and have a relationship with Him. But that plan for you requires that you recognize the sins in your life, the things you've done that you know are wrong and that separate you from Him.

Scripture reminds you that everyone has sinned and has not come up to God's standards (Romans 3:23). So you are not alone. But even more, God offers the opportunity for you to be even closer to Him. And He asks you to believe that Jesus Christ is the One sent to save you. He asks you to believe that nothing and no one else could do that. And He promises that when you believe in Jesus Christ, who was sent just for you, you will no longer be lost in sin but instead will be found in Him. So, Dad, Scripture asks you to do exactly one thing to assure that you are no longer lost but are found: God asks that you say, out loud, that Jesus Christ is Lord. Romans 10:9 says if you confess with your mouth, "Jesus is Lord," and believe in your heart that God raised Him from the dead, you will be saved.

Dad, once you believe and say you believe, you are saved from those sins—you are now a son of God. You were made to have a relationship with your heavenly Father. If you haven't been sure of it yet, today is a very good day to begin that relationship.

LET'S PRAY

Lord, this dad feels lost. You are a faithful God in that You sent Your Son, Jesus Christ, to save this particular dad. And You said that if this dad would call out for Your hope, Your peace, and Your salvation, You would give it without hesitation. This dad is reading this page right now and he believes exactly one thing: that only Jesus can save him. Send Your Holy Spirit to touch his heart to ask for what only Jesus can do. In Jesus' name we pray. Amen.

CONTINUE THE CONNECTION

If you confessed that Jesus Christ is Lord today for the first time, tell someone! Your heavenly Father and all of heaven are celebrating with you today.

16

TONIGHT WE PRAY FOR THE DAD WHO WONDERS WHY BAD THINGS HAPPEN

*I*t is painful when really bad things happen to people we love. They didn't deserve it, and, still, evil came to them. Scripture tells us that Adam was in the garden of Eden to protect it, to keep it, to make sure that everything went along smoothly. That everything would be successful. But God told him there was one rule, one exception, to Adam's management.

Genesis 2:16–17 recounts, "The LORD God commanded the man, 'You are free to eat from any tree of the garden, but you must not eat from the tree of the knowledge of good and evil, for on the day you eat from it, you will certainly die.'" God told Adam that not only would he die but that all of humanity would die. This change from eternal life, which they experienced in the garden, to spiritual and physical death would affect every generation to follow. They would be literally changed from living people to dying people. But also completely and irrevocably. Within themselves, they were broken down to their very DNA. As long as they didn't eat from this tree, they understood exactly what God wanted and how to make everything good. Once they disobeyed God's one rule, they would no longer hear God speak clearly.

Dad, the things that happen in this world that just couldn't have been in God's plan were done by people who were broken. God never intended famine; He never intended disease. But these came into the world because the people were no longer perfectly like God. The people were no longer eternally healthy, so sickness came and spread among them. Evil of all sorts came because people were so separated from God that they no longer felt His goodness at all. Even the things that have happened to you and your family came about because people are still broken. God weeps for you that you must suffer what is so clearly not intended for you. But He is still good in every aspect, and You must trust that He wants to restore His children completely.

LET'S PRAY

Lord, this dad cares for this world like You do. He believes that You have a plan for his life and that it can happen when he keeps his eyes on You. He also knows that You want to restore all of Your children to complete wholeness and health through Your Son, Jesus Christ. Remind him that You are good and You're still in charge of his world. In Jesus' name we pray. Amen.

CONTINUE THE CONNECTION

Take a moment to consider God's goodness even
in the midst of the brokenness of the world.

17

TONIGHT WE PRAY FOR THE DAD WHO IS SLOW TO SPEAK

$\mathcal{D}$ad, we live in a highly charged world filled with lots of emotion. Sometimes on social media it seems as if the main emotion is anger. People today believe very strongly in their own way of life and how they live it. We sometimes feel threatened by differences of opinion. And we have spent a lifetime believing the truth of our own convictions.

James also lived in such a world. The culture of his day included conversations with words coming at a high rate of speed and even higher volume. The ability to make your point would often decide whether you would prevail. And if you thought you were going to lose your point, you might resort to anger to suggest that you were the more righteous, or the more believable, or the more correct. You see, this culture valued being right ahead of solving a problem. And this would often translate from the marketplace into the church environment. It didn't matter what the outcome was, so long as you were right.

James 1:19 says, "My dearly loved brothers, understand this: Everyone must be quick to hear, slow to speak, and slow to anger."

James reminded the church that they (and we) should set ourselves apart in order to be heard. That we should be known for our conversation and how we interact with others. That we should not engage in the type of conversation that is full of fast talk and anger. This matters not only in the church but also with our families. Our most important words are spoken to them. We know James had to teach the Jewish people that it was important to be slow to speak. We can infer this is because this is a hard lesson that doesn't come easily or naturally. However, it's important that we do it. We must practice listening before speaking, because if we get all the way to anger, our voices are no longer heard and the words lose their power.

LET'S PRAY

Lord, this dad wants to speak life with his words. His words represent his heart, and he knows that out of the abundance of his heart, his mouth speaks. He also knows that he must hear his family because only then can he understand them and know what he can say or do to meet their needs. Please help him be measured in his voice so his true heart can emerge. In Jesus' name we pray. Amen.

CONTINUE THE CONNECTION

Dad, take some time to practice taking a pause before you respond. Whether it is to your spouse, your children, your coworkers, or a person online, breathe, and speak slowly and intentionally.

18

TONIGHT WE PRAY FOR THE DAD WHO KNOWS THE HARDEST ASSIGNMENTS CARRY THE GREATEST REWARDS

*M*any times the tasks that appear the easiest turn out to be some of the hardest work we've ever done. And often the greatest results come from these unexpected hard assignments.

In Genesis 11:31, Abram is introduced as being the head of a family that decided to go from Ur of the Chaldees to the land of Canaan. Genesis 12:1–2 says, "The LORD had said to Abram, 'Leave your native country, your relatives, and your father's family, and go to the land that I will show you. I will make you into a great nation. I will bless you and make you famous, and you will be a blessing to others'" (NLT).

Ur was the type of place that no one would have left on a whim. Yet Abram had been a man God spoke to and led. Like most of us when we seek God, Abram wanted God to meet him where he was, showing up in his day-to-day life. But God wanted obedience. God wanted Abram to go. Abram likely didn't dream that God would give him such a monumental task in order to be face-to-face with Him. But what came from this task to leave and go and follow influenced the rest of humanity. You might remember that one of Abram's descendants, Jesus, would eventually come to redeem humanity back to God through Abram's obedience.

Listen, Dad: we don't always know what a conversation with God is going to entail. But if we are always looking for the path of least resistance, we'll miss the greatest blessings. We must listen for what He is actually asking us to do. We must then be brave enough to do it.

LET'S PRAY

Lord, You know that it's the uphill climb that proves the engine. Anyone can take a foot off the gas and point the vehicle when it's going downhill. But it's the wise dad who doesn't coast or shirk from opportunities. He keeps his foot on the gas. This dad knows these assignments make him better. Lord, this dad seeks after Your guidance to reach higher and higher every day. Give him Your strength to accept every assignment, no matter how hard. In Jesus' name we pray. Amen.

CONTINUE THE CONNECTION

As you pray this week, take time to listen for what God is asking you to do. Think back on moments when the task wasn't easy, but He met you just the same.

19

TONIGHT WE PRAY FOR THE DAD WHO HAS EXPERIENCED LOSS

$\mathcal{D}$ad, what do you do when you do everything right and it all falls apart? What do you do when everything you've worked for, everything you've dreamed about, and everything you have is taken away from you? I am here to tell you that there is a place to stand in the midst of the rubble of your life—that you will survive and become even better than you believe possible.

Scripture tells us that Job was a man who had much wealth. Not just wealth; he had it all. He had a perfect reputation, and he was favored by God. Job 1:1 says, "There was a man in the country of Uz named Job. He was a man of perfect integrity, who feared God and turned away from evil." His reputation likely came from his ability and willingness to do everything necessary for everyone he knew. We can see this in his character described throughout the rest of his book. Most of all, he had a family he cherished. They lived together in harmony. And just to make sure they remained true to themselves and to God who had provided for them, Job prayed earnestly for them. He wanted to keep them safe and joyous all together. And then everything was gone. The house, the wealth, the children, everything gone.

The first thing Job did was remind himself that God was greater than everything Job had. God was greater than any storm of calamity that could come his way. And he reminded himself that the God who had provided everything to Job in the first place was certainly able to restore everything Job had lost.

Job had questions just like you do, Dad. He wondered if he'd failed. He wondered if he'd made some big mistake and it was all just now catching up to him. He wondered if he was a man God could bless. At the end of the story, while Job was asking God all of those questions, God revealed Himself to Job in a mighty way. And God restored so much of what he had lost. But the most important lesson from the story of Job is that Job maintained his relationship with God with integrity.

LET'S PRAY

Lord, this dad has experienced his own devastating loss. The only place he has left is his relationship with You. The opinions of others don't matter. Just the trust he has for You can help him go on. Please show Yourself strong to this dad as You did to Job in the midst of his great loss. In Jesus' name we pray. Amen.

CONTINUE THE CONNECTION

This week in your prayer, consider how God continues to be faithful to you in your own healing from loss.

20

TONIGHT WE PRAY FOR THE DAD WHO NEEDS ANSWERS

*E*verything you will ever need to know, God already knows. Every question you will ever ask, God already has an answer for. And that really big situation you're facing right now? He's ready to tell you what to do next.

James 1:5 reminds us, "If any of you lacks wisdom, he should ask God, who gives to all generously and without criticizing, and it will be given to him." James tells us here that God gives wisdom freely, in abundance, and does not question our request. He doesn't criticize what we believe we are lacking. Rather, we are guaranteed wisdom.

In this passage, James was speaking to both Jews and new Christians. Jews were God's chosen people who had been given the Law to follow. These Jewish people were used to looking for specific answers in the Law. If they had a question, they could find the answer there. James was also speaking to new believers of Jesus who hadn't previously been Jews. These Gentiles had no history with the Jewish law but had heard the teachings of Jesus. James was telling both groups that they would come into situations where they didn't know what to do or what proper scriptural perspective to take when they had problems. So James told both groups that they should not rely on the Law and instead remember how they came to faith in Jesus Christ. They should look to those examples of what Jesus said for their answers. And in those circumstances, where it seemed there was no answer, God would provide whatever they needed.

Throughout Scripture we see wisdom as an attribute of God's Spirit. When we ask for wisdom, God Himself comes. He doesn't just send the answers. He shows up, and the answers are found in Him. The same is true for everything you're facing. You might be used to finding answers on your own, but God wants you to seek Him, knowing that He will give His Spirit freely to all who ask.

LET'S PRAY

Lord, this dad needs wisdom because his life is stressful, and he knows he doesn't have all the answers. But that doesn't change his desire to be wise for his children. Give this dad wisdom to see the best outcome and the courage to implement it. Help him lean into the Holy Spirit for guidance. In Jesus' name we pray. Amen.

CONTINUE THE CONNECTION

Are you looking everywhere but to God for your answers? Take a moment to ask God for wisdom, trusting that He will answer you and give it freely.

21

TONIGHT WE PRAY FOR THE DAD WHO WORKS WITH HIS HANDS

$\mathcal{M}$ark 6:2–3 tells us a story about Jesus, who wasn't just a man of great words but was also a man of fine works. On one particular Sabbath, Jesus began teaching in the synagogue. Those who heard Him were amazed. "Where did this man get these things?" they asked. "What's this wisdom that has been given him? What are these remarkable miracles he is performing? Isn't this the carpenter? Isn't this Mary's son and the brother of James, Joseph, Judas and Simon? Aren't his sisters here with us?" (NIV).

Scripture tells us that Jesus worked with His hands. He was a carpenter. It was not wealthy work, but it was valuable to the community. In this profession, Jesus would have known all the local tradesmen and understood their needs. Not just in Nazareth where He was raised but also in the surrounding cities and towns. It was very physical labor; He would have had to work from dawn to dusk because the tradesmen in smaller communities were much poorer. Yet the things Jesus made were valuable. A carpenter made beams for houses, he made yokes for plowing in the fields, and he made wheels for the carts that every single household would have needed for their daily routines.

So the people were astonished that such teaching came from a man who worked day and night to provide for His mother and His brothers and sisters. The people even wondered how Jesus could work with His hands the way He did and still be able to use them for miracles.

Dad, Jesus shows us that God can use us just the way He has made us. You may work from dawn to dusk, but know that God has a plan for you in His kingdom. Whether you are a man who works with your hands professionally or simply out of hobby, this is just one more way you are like Jesus. Through this work you can encounter and connect with the Father's love for you as His son.

LET'S PRAY

Lord, this dad's work may be hard physical labor, but he doesn't shirk from it. When he works, he creates something of value—for himself, for his family, or for someone else. It's something he can be proud of. And that's the way he wants it, to do the hard work because it always counts. Strengthen this dad's hands and heart to continue his labor for You. In Jesus' name we pray. Amen.

CONTINUE THE CONNECTION

This week as you work, consider Jesus working alongside you.

22

TONIGHT WE PRAY FOR THE DAD WHO KNOWS HE CAN COUNT ON GOD

*Y*ou have a history with God. There have been times when He has proven Himself faithful to you. He has shown up when you needed Him to, and He has reminded you that together you can face anything that comes. There is a familiar story in the Scriptures about a young man named David who, because he had seen God strengthen him in the past, anticipated success when he took on the role of giant killer.

You likely know this story. When young David stood face-to-face with Goliath, he said, "The LORD who rescued me from the paw of the lion and the paw of the bear will rescue me from the hand of this Philistine" (1 Samuel 17:37). When we think of this battle, we may remember how David was offered and refused a suit of armor sufficient to protect him from the giant warrior and his weapons. We may remember that the king, Saul, for whom David was battling, had little confidence in a successful outcome. But we might not remember that David knew something the skeptical king did not. David had a history of defeating lions and bears while defending his sheep as a shepherd.

He had the resolve to defend what needed to be protected, and this giant threatening God's people was no different. David might have appeared to be an untrained warrior, but the Lord was with him before, and David knew the Lord would be with him again.

Dad, as you anticipate success in what you will face next, be reminded of the previous giants you have successfully conquered in your story. No matter what outward appearances might indicate, you have in fact been preparing for this next challenge for your entire life. Every moment God has been faithful to see you through a trial, He has been preparing you to take on the next battle ahead of you. Each trial has created a history with God that you can count on.

LET'S PRAY

Lord, You have given this dad success in many endeavors in his life. You have given him small victories in anticipation of even greater ones for him to accomplish. Remind him of those times and help him remember that no matter how great the giant is that he is facing, this dad is an even greater warrior for his family's sake. In Jesus' name we pray. Amen.

CONTINUE THE CONNECTION

This week as you pray, consider these two questions:
What is the giant in front of you? How has God
already shown you that you can defeat it?

23

TONIGHT WE PRAY FOR THE DAD WHO HONORS HIS PARENTS

Scripture tells us in Exodus 20:12, "Honor your father and your mother so that you may have a long life in the land that the LORD your God is giving you." These are not just words, Dad. *Honoring* does not mean just reminding our parents how special they are, how much they mean to us, and what wonderful grandparents they have been. We can't choose to honor our parents only if they were honorable. Honoring our parents means honoring God. Period.

When God placed you into a family, your parents were charged with the responsibility of providing all your needs, whether or not they accepted this responsibility fully. More specifically, they were to invest their time, their provision, and their knowledge and wisdom into your life. More importantly, they were to instruct you in the ways of parenting. As soon as you became a dad, you stepped into that same awesome responsibility. We honor our parents most when we choose to take the wisdom, skills, and knowledge of what we have learned and apply it back to their lives. As they become older and no longer able to take care of themselves in the way they once did, we invest our time and our resources so they can be secure.

In this, we are fulfilling the command. We are recognizing who we have grown to be and taking all the best things that have come from our parents (whether we learned them because we had good examples or we learned them because we lacked the example and wanted to be better) and turning back to our parents with love and support.

Because you have followed the Lord's lead, you will be that dad who honors God. As you grew in wisdom and stature with God and man, like Jesus in Luke 2:52, you became the man and the dad you are today. And as you honor your parents, you raise your children to see the importance of honoring theirs.

LET'S PRAY

Lord, this dad loves his parents. And in his own time and in his own way, he has honored them and recognized their importance in his lives. He realizes there are times and circumstances in which their needs will increase and his importance to them will increase as well. Help this dad truly honor his parents so he can be the best dad he can be in his own children's lives. In Jesus' name we pray. Amen.

CONTINUE THE CONNECTION

Take some time to reach out to your parents this week.
How can you show them honor and respect?

24

TONIGHT WE PRAY FOR THE
DAD WHO REBUILDS

I have friends who like to restore cars. I have other friends who like to restore houses. Many times we like to restore things because they are broken or because fixing something usually costs less than buying it new. But I think many enjoy the challenge of a fixer-upper because we enjoy the process of building something that is better than what was there before.

In the book of Nehemiah, the walls of the city of Jerusalem were in ruins and the people of Israel were in exile in the land of Babylon. Nehemiah the prophet was in the presence of the king of Babylon when an amazing conversation took place. The king asked him,

"Why does your face look so sad when you are not ill?" . . . Then I prayed to the God of heaven, and I answered the king, "If it pleases the king and if your servant has found favor in his sight, let him send me to the city in Judah where my ancestors are buried so that I can rebuild it." (Nehemiah 2:2, 4–5 NIV)

The story goes on to say that the king not only granted Nehemiah the permission to go and rebuild the wall but gave him help to accomplish this task. Like Nehemiah, when parts of our lives need to be restored, grace comes over us to face the challenge, and we have help through the Holy Spirit to accomplish what must be done. God is the Great Builder. He's the One who built the universe by speaking it into existence; and then, when sin entered and His creation was separated, He sent His Son into the world so a bridge might be built back to Himself. God cares about what needs to be restored in your life, and He will help you accomplish the task.

LET'S PRAY

Lord, please remind this dad that You are with him and provide for him even when it looks like his life is in shambles. Remind him that You sent Your Son, Jesus, for his salvation and the Holy Spirit to guide him through the rebuilding process. You stand with him in all circumstances. Please help him take on whatever lies ahead tomorrow. In Jesus' name we pray. Amen.

CONTINUE THE CONNECTION

As you pray this week, think of the circumstances or relationships in your life where, like Nehemiah, you need restoration. Ask the Lord to help you rebuild in those areas.

25

TONIGHT WE PRAY FOR THE
DAD WHO ISN'T WEALTHY

Let's cut to the chase. Not everyone who effectively serves God is wealthy. In our society, and sometimes even in our Christian culture, there is a prevailing notion that service to the Lord begins and ends with how much we can contribute or how much we can provide to others.

There are far too many contradicting examples in Scripture for that mind-set to be true. When criticized, Jesus once made an example of His cousin, John the Baptist, saying, "What did you go out into the wilderness to see? A reed swaying in the wind? What then did you go out to see? A man dressed in soft clothes? Look, those who wear soft clothes are in kings' palaces" (Matthew 11:7–8).

Listen—John the Baptist had nothing. Really, just nothing. He ate locusts and honey on purpose. He chose to have nothing because he didn't want anything to get in the way of him spreading God's word to the people. He baptized thousands because people heard God in his words and actions. His simple and effective demeanor caused those thousands to repent of their sins that they might turn back to God. Where the religious structure of the day seemed to suggest that God was angry with the people and they could never measure up, John told them that the simple act of repenting could begin to change God's heart. And just like now, people wondered why John wasn't wealthy or provisioned or "dressed in soft clothes." Jesus reminded everyone around Him that there was no one more effective than John in leading people to God.

Dad, you have value in the kingdom of God. You might not speak to stadiums full of people. You might not baptize hundreds. But you may have an opportunity to speak to someone dressed in blue jeans and a T-shirt while you look the exact same way, and you could change their life.

LET'S PRAY

Lord, this dad just wants an opportunity to do his best for You. He doesn't want to worry about how he looks or what his bank balance looks like. Remind him that You sometimes use the least of us to do the most for the rest of us. He already has all he needs to be used by You. Help him see just how much he has. In Jesus' name we pray. Amen.

CONTINUE THE CONNECTION

Pause to thank the Lord for helping you
build His kingdom and not yours.

26

TONIGHT WE PRAY FOR THE DAD WHO MIGHT BE AWAY FOR SOME TIME

*A*s my children grew up, they always looked for my return. Whether I was going to work or to the grocery store, they loved when I came back. My hope was that no matter how long I had to be away, they knew I would always rather be with them.

On numerous occasions, Jesus explained to His disciples that He would eventually have to leave in order to fulfill His calling. But He promised them that it would be okay, saying, "Your heart must not be troubled. Believe in God; believe also in Me. In My Father's house are many dwelling places; if not, I would have told you. I am going away to prepare a place for you" (John 14:1–2). Even though Jesus said words like these, and even though He specifically told his disciples that He would have to be crucified, they could not accept the premise that Jesus would ever be absent from them. When He did eventually die on the cross, rise from the dead, and then ascend into heaven, suddenly, even as grown men, Jesus' disciples felt lost.

Jesus had told them He had to go and would return at some future date or they never would be able to accomplish His mission or theirs. They had to believe that the Father had prepared a place in His heart and in heaven for them and that Jesus was not leaving them so much as He was securing their future reward for a job well done.

As a dad, you hope to never be required to leave your children for an extended period of time, but sometimes obligations take us away. Scripture teaches us to be like Jesus and to live out what He modeled. Jesus Himself modeled a life that took Him away from those He loved in order to fulfill the calling of His heavenly Father and to prepare for their future.

LET'S PRAY

Lord, we pray for the dad who wishes he could be there for one more story or one more drink of water. He has to miss so many things that are important to his children, and he has only so much time. He desperately hopes they will understand why he has to be absent. Please give this dad peace so he might know that You are protecting sensitive hearts and minds as they sleep. In Jesus' name we pray. Amen.

CONTINUE THE CONNECTION

This week as you pray, remember that you are securing your children's future and speak a blessing over it. As their dad, it is okay to pray over every aspect of that future—including health, career, and even your future grandchildren.

27

TONIGHT WE PRAY FOR THE DAD WHO LIVES IN CHRONIC PHYSICAL PAIN

Scripture reports many instances of suffering. With the exception of those dying for their faith, probably no record is found of any more suffering physically for the gospel than what the apostle Paul endured. Paul said in 2 Corinthians 11:24–25, "Five times I received 39 lashes from Jews. Three times I was beaten with rods by the Romans. Once I was stoned by my enemies. Three times I was shipwrecked. I have spent a night and a day in the open sea." Paul had suffered.

To understand how greatly he suffered, know that instances of thirty-nine lashes with whips were so severe that the prevailing wisdom of the day suggested forty lashes would kill a young man. A Roman beating with rods could continue until a person was unconscious. And stoning was a punishment that usually included numerous broken bones and nerve damage to the spine. And yet Paul persevered.

He praised the Lord for giving him the opportunity to suffer for Him. Paul knew that his body did not determine his value to the Lord. And, Dad, you know the same. The Lord has not wished on you the trials you have suffered. He would always have you to be in health and wholeness as He originally designed for you in the garden at creation. However, Scripture says that the Lord's arm is not too short to reach His children and heal them from their diseases. Not just things like measles or pneumonia but also where your body is dis-eased—a sore back, an aching head, an area or a system that needs to be restored. Even as you journey toward healing, God will affirm to the uttermost your ability to live your life for Him.

LET'S PRAY

Lord, this dad suffers mightily, and he wonders if he can withstand it. Some days treatment is effective and some days it isn't. All he knows is that he's suffering through merely doing the things he was supposed to do, and now he can't do those things or a host of others. You know him and You know his circumstances. You have prepared him for a life that he did not expect, but You have also prepared a way for him to see ways he can take care of his family. Open his eyes to the new possibilities. In Jesus' name we pray. Amen.

CONTINUE THE CONNECTION

Like Paul, you continue to praise God despite all your suffering. This week, take a moment to ask God to give you a continued sense of purpose for His kingdom.

28

TONIGHT WE PRAY FOR THE DAD
WHO WORKS LONG HOURS

Scripture relates a story about how the disciple Peter met Jesus. Simon Peter was a good fisherman. Once, in the early days of Jesus' ministry, Jesus came upon two boats being cleaned along with fishermen's gear and nets. One of these boats belonged to Peter, and Jesus asked if He might use his boat to speak from, since the crowds would gather around Jesus, making it difficult to teach. After Jesus had finished speaking, he turned to Peter and suggested that he go out a little way and let down his net.

Luke 5:5 records Peter's response: "'Master,' Simon replied, 'we've worked hard all night long and caught nothing! But at Your word, I'll let down the nets.'" Peter had a challenge right there. He had done this so long that he knew in the natural world nothing good was going to come from doing what Jesus had asked him. Would he be willing to go the extra step just because Jesus asked? In this uncertain circumstance, Peter complied. And Scripture reports that the net brought in such a catch that the other fishermen had to come with their freshly cleaned boats and nets to help bring it in.

As a dad, you do hard work for long hours. Whether you work outside of the house or take care of your family from within your home, you give it your all. Like Peter, there may be moments when at the end of the day you are just ready to be done. However, also like Peter, you know that when Jesus asks you to follow His Word, it will always bring reward. There might be days when you say, "I've worked all day, and have nothing to show for it, but at Your Word, I'll do as You say. I'll follow Your command. I'll take the extra step. I'll help my neighbor, or I'll help with homework." You can rest assured that when you do, you'll see Jesus do what only He can. He'll bring in a great catch from your obedience.

LET'S PRAY

Lord, this dad works hard, and there aren't always enough hours to spend with his children. Sometimes, like Peter, he's tired—but he makes the effort because he's committed to them. They count on him, and he never wants to let them down. Just as You multiplied the fish in Peter's nets, multiply this dad's time so his work and his home life can be productive. Give him new eyes to see his time opportunities even better. In Jesus' name we pray. Amen.

CONTINUE THE CONNECTION

This week, pay attention to the moments Jesus might be asking you to cast your nets or give your time to something unexpected. God always blesses obedience.

29

TONIGHT WE PRAY FOR THE DAD WHO CREATES FOR HIS FAMILY

*G*enesis 2:15 says, "The LORD God took the man and placed him in the garden of Eden to work it and watch over it." Dad, your heavenly Father designed you to work. That could be hard to hear, perhaps. But His point is that He wants you to achieve. And we do that as we work. You might think of work as simply what you do to contribute financially, but work is so much more than that. Working is creating, completing, producing, or restoring. As you do this, you have the privilege of fulfilling exactly what God told you to do. And as you are working, you are exercising God's authority over your world and exhibiting God's power within it.

Remember, God doesn't love us based on our performance. While He wants us to honor Him with our work, our position as His children is secure even when we don't. It's not important to God how hard you work. It is important to God that you want to achieve in order to honor His calling. It's important to Him that you want to do what He has called you to do, whatever that might be. In the story of creation, God created man and woman, Adam and Eve, to watch over their environment and to make it better. God gave them explicit instructions on how to manage it. He wanted them to have joy over the privilege of taking care of it. He wanted them to want to take care of it. And He gave them the authority to accomplish that. He told them that everything they saw was theirs to manage.

Dad, here's where you come in. God was exercising a fatherly role in creating this world for you. As He created, He worked. We know that on the seventh day, He rested "from all His works" (Hebrews 4:4). And now He invites you to join Him in creating for your family. Just as He made the world you live in, you are creating a world your children live in, and you aren't doing it alone. The Lord calls you to work alongside Him and to rest alongside Him.

LET'S PRAY

Lord, this dad loves his fatherly role. He is determined to do what he believes You have asked him to do. His children recognize their dad's authority and spiritual stature because he conducts his life with the assurance that God is with him. Honor his faith in You every day and with greater blessings. In Jesus' name we pray. Amen.

CONTINUE THE CONNECTION

As you go about your tasks this week, think of each one as an assignment from the Lord. He is laboring with you.

30

TONIGHT WE PRAY FOR THE
DAD WHO IS HOPEFUL

*W*hen you became a dad, you suddenly became the most hopeful person on the planet. This was an exciting event. A living person was born to you and your spouse, or placed into your heart by adoption, and you now had the opportunity to raise a child you hoped would change the world. Because that's what we want, isn't it? We'd like to change the world—and if we can't, we hope our children can.

The moment we become dads, the life we're living is suddenly not ours. In many ways, we put our own life aside and learn to live it for our children. And it isn't easy in the beginning. It takes practice. So you're going to grow up, no matter how old you are, and mature and become a better dad every day. And the hoping begins. You hope because you've never done this before. Most of all, you hope you will be able to do this with the success that comes only through Christ.

Scripture says that love "bears all things, believes all things, hopes all things, endures all things" (1 Corinthians 13:7). You love this child with all your heart, soul, and strength. And based on that love, the first thing you have to do, according to Scripture, is believe. You're going to have to believe that God loves your child even more than you do. And you're going to have to believe that He wants you to succeed in raising a child who will change the world. And then, Dad, after you've loved and you've believed, you have to hope. Sometimes hope means looking into the future with nothing but the horizon out there. But then you notice that right over that horizon is the Lord. And you and that child of yours are going to start walking until you get to Him.

LET'S PRAY

Lord, this dad has hopes for his children. He hopes they will see him and want to be like him as they see Jesus in him. As Paul had hopes for the church at Corinth, so also does this dad hope that his children will achieve even more than he has. And he knows that he can never stop hoping and praying for their success, no matter where they are. Give this dad peace as he hopes for everything good. In Jesus' name we pray. Amen.

CONTINUE THE CONNECTION

What are you hoping for your children? Pause to pray about these hopes, trusting God has a good future in store for your kids.

31

TONIGHT WE PRAY FOR THE DAD WHO ACCEPTS HELP

*O*kay, Dad. Sometimes we have a difficult time accepting help. We're the ones who do the helping. We reach the top shelf; we get rid of the spider; we open the jar. We listen and give wisdom. We may be sharing the family responsibilities today, but we've always seen ourselves as the one who gets things done, whatever that looks like in our homes. So what do we do when we are the ones who need help? I'll admit, it can be hard.

Scripture tells a story about Moses leading the children of Israel against the Amalekites. These were bad dudes in God's eyes because they had initially prevented His people from getting to the promised land. And Moses was God's man. Moses thought that if there was going to be a battle won, Moses was going to have to represent God. So as the battle raged, Moses held up the staff that God had used to part the Red Sea.

Exodus 17:11–12 describes what happened:

While Moses held up his hand, Israel prevailed, but whenever he put his hand down, Amalek prevailed. . . . Then Aaron and Hur supported his hands, one on one side and one on the other so that his hands remained steady until the sun went down.

On this occasion, instead of God vanquishing the enemy, Aaron and Hur, seeing what Moses needed, moved in to help their leader accomplish his responsibility to lead his people and win the battle.

Listen, Dad, we have a tendency to think, in times of great personal hardship, that God will just fix everything. He might, or He might also send an Aaron and Hur to help you complete your project. And you should accept God's help in whatever form or fashion it arrives. Sometimes His help doesn't look like what you might expect.

LET'S PRAY

Lord, this dad has always been a winner in Your eyes. And he's won many battles with Your strength. He knows there is help available, but he just hasn't always accepted it. You always have resources available to meet this dad's needs. Open his eyes to the opportunities for victory that he hasn't always seen or even looked for, and prepare him for the next battle. This dad knows You will send just the help he needs. In Jesus' name we pray. Amen.

CONTINUE THE CONNECTION

Who helps you most? Take a moment to thank God for them.

32

TONIGHT WE PRAY FOR THE DAD WHO WORKS HARD FOR HIS FAMILY

*A*s dads, we want to provide for our families. What we do isn't just for the sake of a paycheck or to fill the hours in our day. We work hard because that's one way we show our families love. Great dads are devoted and meet the spiritual and emotional needs of those in our care. We are also determined to do our best to provide for and protect them from the world.

It's why you keep going. You get up in the morning without reservation or complaint. That's your attitude because you know that reservation or complaint accomplishes nothing, and you are about making good decisions. So you grab your laptop or your hammer, or you get about making breakfast for the kids. That's love. Even in seasons when you do not have a job, that does not change your heart to care for your family.

Your love gives strength for weakness. You give determination for delay. You give your all because you know that God gave you this specific family for a reason. He knew that you were and continue to be the perfect dad for them. Not because you're perfect, but because He is. And because you are dedicated to making sure His love shows up in your home daily.

Jesus said in John 15:13, "No one has greater love than this, that someone would lay down his life for his friends." Jesus was talking about going to the cross on our behalf, but He wasn't just talking about His love for us. He was talking about our love for each other. You may not think that what you do is special—that every dad works hard and gives his all. But you willingly give up your life, your daily agenda, and your expectations. You lay down your life for those you love, and that puts Christ's love on display in your home. That's why you keep moving forward, Dad. That's really why you work so hard.

LET'S PRAY

Lord, bless the work of this dad's hands. He understands that everything he does has purpose as he represents Jesus on a daily basis. Bless him and his family through his work. And as he finishes today, give him peace that he has been successful so he can begin again tomorrow. In Jesus' name we pray. Amen.

CONTINUE THE CONNECTION

As you go about your work this week, consider how you are showing God's love to those around you and to your family. Your daily sacrifice has a great reward. What you do is important.

33

TONIGHT WE PRAY FOR THE DAD WHO APPRECIATES HIS CHURCH FAMILY

*A*re you a part of your local body of believers? It could be a church, a life group, a Sunday school class, or a home group with which you have a close family relationship. Unity, trust, love, and connection as believers in Christ are the cornerstones of this community. In this way, these relationships are often similar to a family unit.

In the Scriptures, we find Paul the apostle having just such a relationship with the church at Philippi. It is widely held that after Paul's salvation on the Damascus road, he went into the desert for seventeen years to prepare for his ministry (Galatians 1:17–18; 2:1). When he returned, the first place he ministered was Philippi. Since this was the very beginning of his ministry, his feelings were very deep toward this group. In a manner of speaking, it was as though they had grown up together. So they shared their blessings and their trials together. And because the believers there had been so close, together in unity, and so trusting in Paul because of his love for them, they often sent him gifts to keep his ministry going. Paul loved the church at

Philippi as if they were his family. When he spoke to them the words of Philippians 1:6, "I am sure of this, that He who started a good work in you will carry it on to completion until the day of Christ Jesus," it was his deep affection for them.

Dad, much of Scripture can be understood in the light of family—family such as brothers and sisters and children and wise fathers. It is a good thing to have a church that is like family. Whether we are gathered in a building or in your home, or we are meeting remotely, we learn and we grow, we encourage and we hold up one another when we are in a family of believers. I have a feeling you're not the type of dad to overlook the importance of this community.

LET'S PRAY

Lord, this dad loves his church family. They've been through great trials and great joys together. They've learned to lean on each other. Lord, as he brings his children up in his faith, keep their relationship strong and centered in You. Help his relationship with his church family continue to grow. In Jesus' name we pray. Amen.

CONTINUE THE CONNECTION

Staying connected with like-hearted men is important.
Take a minute this week to connect with someone
in your church family who shares your faith.

34

TONIGHT WE PRAY FOR THE DAD WHO KNOWS THAT LIFE IS FULL OF STRUGGLES

*T*he gospel of Matthew relates a story involving Jesus' disciple Peter and a number of Peter's friends. They all were returning from a missionary trip when Jesus and these men had miraculously fed five thousand people and their families. Jesus had decided He needed to pray separately for a while. So He sent the disciples on ahead to make the journey across the Sea of Galilee alone.

Peter was an experienced fisherman in these waters, and he knew squalls could come up quickly and without warning. Unfortunately, one did, and the fishermen struggled together in the dark. They were only a mile from their starting place, but they were tired from the long day. Even in the dark from the shore, Jesus could see their struggles.

Suddenly, Jesus walked up to the men and said, as recorded in Matthew 14:27–30, "Have courage! It is I. Don't be afraid."

"Lord, if it's You," Peter answered Him, "command me to come to You on the water."

"Come!" He said.

And climbing out of the boat, Peter started walking on the water and came toward Jesus. But when he saw the strength of the wind, he was afraid. And beginning to sink, he cried out, "Lord, save me!"

The fishermen did not expect to see Jesus, but when He walked on the water up to their boat, Peter knew they could be saved from their struggles. He knew that with Jesus, even out in the midst of the waves, he'd experience a complete salvation from the storm. Likewise, when Jesus offers us relief, we should always be willing to receive it—whether or not it makes sense. Because it is in His presence that our struggles cease, even if the wind and waves do not.

LET'S PRAY

Lord, this dad has experienced struggles, and he's sometimes felt lost in the wind and the waves of adversity. Please remind him that he is not alone when things are dark; You are always there in the storm. Help him trust that You are watching out for his family and he can rest in You knowing his family is safe. In Jesus' name we pray. Amen.

CONTINUE THE CONNECTION

What is one way that you can walk to Jesus even
in the middle of the storm this week?

35

TONIGHT WE PRAY FOR THE DAD WHO CHOOSES BLESSING

$\mathcal{D}$ad, you make choices every day. You make choices about what you will eat and what you will wear. You make choices about where you might go and what you might do when you get there. You also make choices about how you will respond in any given situation. When the water heater breaks, how will you respond? When your child is disobedient, how will you respond? When money is tight or when money comes unexpectedly, how will you respond?

Scripture says in Deuteronomy 30:19, "I call heaven and earth as witnesses against you today that I have set before you life and death, blessing and curse. Choose life so that you and your descendants may live." Each moment we live in the tension of this choice. Will we bless or will we curse?

Dad, we put a lot of stock into choosing our actions. We know that our actions matter, but we must put just as much effort into choosing how we will view and respond to the circumstances around us. Your words, your actions, and your attitude all matter. You know this. You know your children are watching. We are given the power to bless. We are given the responsibility to rise to the challenge of blessing even when we feel like cursing. When we create a home where blessing is the norm, we aren't just looking on the bright side. We are investing in the hope of our family's future. We are to choose life so that our families may live, not just for today but also for tomorrow. Today, choose to bless.

LET'S PRAY

Lord, this dad knows that choices come every day. He wants to make the wisest decisions. He knows that You've called him for just this time and just this place for his family. And he also knows that You give him the opportunity every day to follow You more closely. He wants even his responses to be Your responses. Grow this dad in wisdom and truth so he can have confidence in his choices. In Jesus' name we pray. Amen.

CONTINUE THE CONNECTION

What do your daily responses teach your family about God? Are you revealing your Father's heart in your attitude? Are you blessing or cursing?

36

TONIGHT WE PRAY FOR THE DAD WHO ISN'T DEFINED BY HIS PAST

*T*he man we know as Paul today was once called Saul. Acts 9:1–2 describes him this way: "Meanwhile, Saul was still breathing threats and murder against the disciples of the Lord. He went to the high priest and requested letters from him to the synagogues in Damascus, so that if he found any men or women who belonged to the Way, he might bring them as prisoners to Jerusalem." Saul was a highly trained student of the Word and totally zealous for God. He believed that everything Jesus and His followers stood for was an affront to God. You see, most early Christians had been Jews, so they came under the authority of the high priest, and therefore, Saul. As long as they were blaspheming God by comparing Jesus to God, Saul believed they should be punished, and he searched far and wide looking for opportunities to persecute them.

As Saul went to Damascus to enlist others to help him persecute the Christians, Jesus appeared to him as a bright light. Acts 9:3–5 records, "A light from heaven suddenly flashed around him. Falling to the ground, he heard a voice saying to him, 'Saul, Saul, why are you persecuting Me?'" Jesus knew Saul, knew his training, knew his understanding of the Word, knew his faithfulness to God. Jesus also loved Saul and knew Saul was the type of man He could use. Saul's life was changed on that road. He went from persecuting Christians to becoming one of the most renowned men to spread the gospel of Jesus Christ. Jesus looked past the fire-breathing Saul and changed his world for God's glory.

No matter who your friends or family or coworkers or community knew you to be in the past, you have permission to grow. God doesn't define you by who you were, but He continually transforms you for His good work.

LET'S PRAY

Lord, this dad has done things he's not proud of. Looking back on his life, he knows he's made some bad decisions that have had ramifications for him and others around him. But that's not his life now. You've always had the answers to the past, the present, and the future. Give this dad a vision of what is to come so he can walk the path that leads to peace. In Jesus' name we pray. Amen.

CONTINUE THE CONNECTION

What do you need to leave behind so you can grow forward?

37

TONIGHT WE PRAY FOR THE DAD WHO KNOWS HE HAS ALL HE NEEDS

We face a world that daily shouts in our face, "You've never had enough, you don't have enough, and you'll never have enough!" But God tells us a completely different story throughout His Word.

In what's called the Sermon on the Mount, recorded in Matthew 6, Jesus taught all those who would listen:

So don't worry, saying, "What will we eat?" or "What will we drink?" or "What will we wear?" For the idolaters eagerly seek all these things, and your heavenly Father knows that you need them. But seek first the kingdom of God and His righteousness, and all these things will be provided for you. (vv. 31–33)

Jesus called "blessed" all those who understood that God had promised to provide for them.

Jesus was telling us that we do not have to struggle for more. When we acknowledge that what we have is everything we need and that He is the One who has provided it to us, we will be blessed. And when we seek His kingdom and put aside the demands of the world, all things shall be added for our good.

It can be hard to keep the main thing the main thing, but you are a dad who does not get distracted by the shouts that call you on a quest for more. You know that *more* is one thing you can never fully possess, because once you have it the line shifts and you are reaching again for what lures you further and further from what you actually need.

Seek first the kingdom. That's what you do every day. Not because of who you are but because of who He is. Through Him, you have all you need.

LET'S PRAY

Lord, this dad trusts You with his blessings. He acknowledges that You are the one who has provided and that He can count on You for future provision. He knows that his work may be stressful, but he's grateful for work. His children may try his patience, but they are a blessing, and he is grateful. He has many blessings, and Your goodness is multiplied abundantly to his family. Show Yourself real in all circumstances to them. In Jesus' name we pray. Amen.

CONTINUE THE CONNECTION

This week as you pray, think of your blessings and take a moment to acknowledge the Giver of all good gifts.

38

TONIGHT WE PRAY FOR THE DAD WHO LONGS FOR UNITY

*W*e all know that some families have a hard time getting along. Maybe different personalities or styles of living or maybe even offense over family issues have caused a separation. This is not uncommon, even among Christian families. Truthfully, if this is not the case for you, it is still important to discuss. It's good to know what the Lord says about these situations, because someone you know may be struggling.

There was a church in Scripture known for its messy squabbles—the church in Corinth. The apostle Paul wrote extensively to this body. It was a church he had spent much time in, and their needs were familiar to him. The fact that there seemed to be some offense entering into their midst disturbed him, and he knew this would fracture the church. In addition, he knew that such a fracture would have long-term consequences for this church and its members. And since the church was so big and so well known, there would have been quite the ripple effect through other Christian communities. It would hurt not only their reputation but also the reputation of other believers. He sent them a beautiful letter of teaching and instruction, and in that letter Paul penned these words: "Now these three remain: faith, hope, and love. But the greatest of these is love" (1 Corinthians 13:13). Paul knew that love could cover a multitude of flaws, differences, and offenses. He knew that love was the foundation of the church.

Dad, love is also the foundation of our family. When we see turmoil and the pain caused by separation and offense, we can apply the healing power of God's love to the situation. He loved us when we were lost in sin, and we show that love to others through compassion and forgiveness.

LET'S PRAY

Lord, this dad loves his family. He understands that sometimes personalities and offense can cause clashes, but at the end of the day, he believes his is a family that loves one another. Now as he prays for unity and connection, we ask that Your love would surround each member. We pray that forgiveness and understanding would be offered and received and that healing would begin. In Jesus' name we pray. Amen.

CONTINUE THE CONNECTION

This week in prayer, bring up any place where disunity has grown in your family and ask the Lord to begin to heal those wounds. He is interested in making everything that concerns you whole and well.

39

TONIGHT WE PRAY FOR THE DAD WHO HAS LOST A CHILD

*N*ot all dads have experienced the loss of a child. Perhaps you are one who has, or perhaps you are a dad who is close to someone who has. This tragedy is far too common, and it pains the heart of our Father in heaven. He has experienced the ache of losing a Son. There is comfort in knowing that we serve a God who isn't far off from our suffering. Sometimes all we can do when we feel deep despair is cry out for Him, trusting He will hear and comfort us. And, Dad, He always does.

The psalmist described a time when King David was afraid for his own life and the lives of those around him. The enemy had conjured up strife for his kingdom; they were closing in, and David's last best response was to cry out to the Lord. He said in Psalm 56:3, "When I am afraid, I will trust in You." Sometimes that's all we can do. When it seems the world is falling apart around us, we can cry out the words of David: "I will trust in You!"

We know that when sin entered the world, so did death. And we know mourning and loss and death are part of this world. And we also know there are no easy answers about death. But in times of abject sorrow, for ourselves or for someone we love, our ever-present hope is Jesus. He understands all our very real sufferings, even if we do not understand them ourselves. As dads, we must lean hard into the goodness of the Lord, always looking for His promise of peace and rest for tomorrow.

LET'S PRAY

Lord, this dad is struggling after the miscarriage, stillbirth, or loss of his child. As a dad, he wants to fix broken things, but when facing the loss of a baby, he cannot fix it. When the doctors did all they could do, what is left for him to do? Sometimes the depth of his own grief prevents him from being the strength his spouse needs to recover from the loss as well. And the pain of this loss spills over into the entire family, as all are affected. This dad needs a supernatural touch of the Holy Spirit and healing for his entire family. Strengthen him as he tries to grieve with faith in You. In Jesus' name we pray. Amen.

CONTINUE THE CONNECTION

If this is something you've experienced, Dad, take some time this week to process your feelings, knowing you serve a God whose own Son died so you could be close to Him.

40

TONIGHT WE PRAY FOR THE DAD
WHO SEES GOD IN NATURE

*G*enesis 1:1 says, "In the beginning God created the heavens and the earth" (NIV). Many of us enjoy nature. Some of us are runners, hikers, or fishermen. We're outdoors because we want to be, whether on a walk or for sport. We experience God's beauty and diversity in what we see. We explore because we want to see places we've never seen or don't see often. We climb different mountains because they represent different challenges. We want to hike trails because they are long and arduous and require us to think about where we are and what we're doing. But importantly, as we are outside, we see all of God's creation. Even more importantly, we should want our children to experience God's greatness in creation as well.

He made all of creation for our enjoyment and so we could experience Him in His creation. We are made better dads when we think about what God has done, but we can see what God has done, feel it, and really know it when we are out in His world. And all the time, God is with us. He tells us as we are climbing that rock, "Isn't this just the best rock to climb?" And when we are hiking that trail, He asks, "Did you ever think just how good it was to put that stream right where you need it the most?" So when we see a sunrise or a sunset, or stand on the edge of an ocean and feel the power of the water as it laps at our feet, we can know that those experiences have been provided for us. And that He loves us.

Dad, the heavens and the earth are created to assure you that God is God. Live in His love and provision as often as you can. And look for Him every day in the world and wonder around you.

LET'S PRAY

Lord, this dad is grateful for Your creation. He knows that everything You do is perfect and right. You chose the way the universe and everything within it would be created for the most good. He knows that You love him, because the universe was, in part, created for him. And now he can see Your love for him in everything around him. Help him continue to focus on Your blessings every day as he encounters the world You made. In Jesus' name we pray. Amen.

CONTINUE THE CONNECTION

As you observe nature this week, remember that the same Lord who called mountains out of the oceans can call what needs to be into being in your life.

41

TONIGHT WE PRAY FOR THE
DAD WHO IS LONELY

*W*e often think about our Savior, Jesus Christ, who suffered in His physical body in ways we cannot possibly imagine. The thorns, the nails, the whipping that exposed His very muscle and bone, all are incomprehensible to us. The loss of blood, the crucifixion that made it impossible to breathe, the hours on the cross itself give us so much pause when we attempt to identify with His suffering. No, we can't imagine it. Yet there is one aspect of Jesus' suffering most of us have experienced.

Separation.

There at the foot of the cross, His family was present, but there had been words of separation between them. He had looked at John and asked him to take care of His mother. He had looked at His mother and told her that John would be like a son to her now. His disciples had fled the scene for all sorts of reasons; perhaps they could not identify with Jesus' suffering and felt incapable of responding in this terrible ordeal. But there was an even deeper separation about to take place.

In Matthew 27:46 we read, "At about three o'clock, Jesus called out with a loud voice, *'Eli, Eli, lema sabachthani?'* which means 'My God, my God, why have you abandoned me?'" (NLT). For us, we try to understand what it meant for Jesus to be separated in that moment from God. But for Jesus, the separation was personal. He was separated from His Father. Can you wrap your heart around that?

The separation you have endured in your life is real, and it is painful. And whether separation has come through death, divorce, deployment, or long hours away from home, Jesus understands. No matter the cause of your loneliness, remember this: you have a Savior who knows the ache of separation. He will walk with you as you take each day as it comes, connecting with your family, remembering you are never alone.

LET'S PRAY

Lord, this dad probably didn't ask for the circumstances surrounding his loneliness, and he needs to know You're with him. Remind him that Jesus went to the cross and endured separation so You could be reunited with him. Strengthen this dad to face tomorrow with courage. In Jesus' name we pray. Amen.

CONTINUE THE CONNECTION

This week as you pray, remember that God understands the loneliness you are feeling and is with you in your time of trouble.

42

TONIGHT WE PRAY FOR THE DAD WHO KNOWS VICTORY AND DEFEAT

I have a feeling you're the type of guy who knows that there will be both victories and defeats, good days and bad ones, moments of hope and times of discouragement. You know that some days the mountain looks higher than others, but you are a guy who has made it to the top and knows what it takes to get there again. You have seen God come through for you. You have felt His support as you climb. And whether you are in a season in the valley or a season on the summit, you know where you're aiming. You know where you are leading your family.

Psalm 30:4–6 says, "Sing the praises of the LORD, you his faithful people; praise his holy name. For his anger lasts only a moment, but his favor lasts a lifetime; weeping may stay for the night, but rejoicing comes in the morning. When I felt secure, I said, 'I will never be shaken'" (NIV).

The psalmist wrote here that we should be in a continual attitude of expectancy for the goodness of the Lord. Sorrow and weeping are temporary. Joy is our aim. Rejoicing in God's favor is our lifeline. We are to expect that God has gone before us and prepared the path that we would use to climb. We should relish the opportunity to ascend to the peak even as we are beginning the journey. We should trust that God has an answer before the problem even arises. Before discouragement attempts to pull us down, there is hope. Before there is an unexpected bill in the midst of a financial crisis, there is a God who provides. Before there is bad news from the doctor, this dad believes there is a God who heals.

God promises that He will meet us. He is preparing us and preparing the next day for victory. Aim for the mountaintop. You'll get there again.

LET'S PRAY

Lord, this dad knows that victory and defeat can seem just seconds apart. He knows that circumstances can convince him that he can't win. And then suddenly, he sees Your goodness. He has seen his tears of weeping for calamity in his family turn to tears of joy for a victory over those trials. This dad is determined to look for and see victory through faith in God. Strengthen his resolve tonight. In Jesus' name we pray. Amen.

CONTINUE THE CONNECTION

Take a moment to make a note of where you are aiming. Don't stay in discouragement or defeat.

43

TONIGHT WE PRAY FOR THE DAD WHO UNIFIES HIS FAMILY IN CRISIS

*J*ehoshaphat was a respected king in Israel who served the Lord in ways that few kings were able to emulate. Known for his generous heart, he sometimes provided for those who did not know the Lord. This caused some dissent within the people because they saw the king as unfaithful to their God. Yet in his generosity, he made sure that the people followed the Lord, even to the extent of removing idols and structures that the people worshipped instead of worshipping God.

As this brought the people together, they understood that the king stood for the people and that their unity would allow them to prosper together. We read a story about King Jehoshaphat in 2 Chronicles 20:2–4:

> People came and told Jehoshaphat, "A vast number from beyond the Dead Sea and from Edom has come to fight against you; . . . Jehoshaphat was afraid, and he resolved to seek the LORD. Then he proclaimed a fast for all Judah, who gathered to seek the LORD.

Consequently, when the Edomites marshalled their forces to attack the army of Jehoshaphat, he knew that the people had become unified in their communities. He declared that the entire nation would repent before the Lord in a fast and that when they did, the Lord would protect them. The Spirit of the Lord came upon those gathered for the fast, and the people were prepared to fight their enemy together.

You have been preparing your family to face crisis together whether you realized it or not. Every moment that brought unity to your family strengthened it. You reminded each other that you could count on one another. You prepared to lean on each other. And when the crisis occurred, like King Jehoshaphat, you knew to call on God together.

LET'S PRAY

Lord, we pray for the dad who keeps unifying his family. You see, he believes that together, and with You, he can meet the challenges that come. He has done what it takes to keep his family focused on the problems ahead. And in times of crisis or calamity, this dad has his eyes keenly focused on You as he plans. Remind him that You always have his back as he continues to press forward for his family. In Jesus' name we pray. Amen.

CONTINUE THE CONNECTION

How are you unifying your family this week? How are they building trust with you and with one another?

44

TONIGHT WE PRAY FOR THE DAD WHO FEELS LIKE TIME IS RUNNING OUT

$\mathcal{S}$ometimes life feels like a sporting event with the clock ticking toward the end of the game. Your children are growing older (whether they are two or twenty-two) and maybe even starting to go their separate ways. You may even feel like you've missed out on some of the milestones in their lives while you were trying to provide everything they needed. You wanted to be available, but it just wasn't possible. We've all felt this way, whether we were working away from the home or around the home trying to keep everything in order.

Here is a secret from further down the road: you never stop being a dad. Until your last breath, you will always be the father to these children. Being a dad is not controlled by time or space. It is always a relationship. No matter what has gone before, or what mistakes you have made, you cannot argue with past events. The past will always be the past. But the past doesn't determine tomorrow. God always calls us into a better, brighter future.

In your mind, you hear that clock ticking. But you need to know that you haven't lost. There is still time left to be a great dad. So keep trying, keep going, keep caring, keep providing, keep praying, keep doing everything you can to excel. Keep showing up at the right time. Keep believing you have what it takes to be the father they need. Everything you do is important and a deposit in your children's future.

Psalm 90:10 says, "Our days may come to seventy years, or eighty, if our strength endures; yet the best of them are but trouble and sorrow, for they quickly pass, and we fly away" (NIV). The concept of time flying, the end of the game, is not new. We all feel the same passage of time. And just as it did for the psalmist, sometimes it seems the sorrow stands out more than the joy. But there are still joys waiting for you, Dad. God has already prepared them for you. There's still time left to enjoy life with your children, whatever that looks like.

LET'S PRAY

Lord, this dad may be looking back with sorrow. He may have regrets about his relationship with his children. He may wish he had been able to be more involved or wish he could be more involved now. He may feel as if the time that has passed is not redeemable, but there's still joy to be found. Help him find it in this next season of his life. In Jesus' name we pray. Amen.

CONTINUE THE CONNECTION

How can you pause to appreciate the time
you have with your children today?

45

TONIGHT WE PRAY FOR THE DAD WHO STRUGGLES WITH TEMPTATIONS

*M*any of us have been tempted, including righteous people in Scripture. It's natural. Our eyes see something we've only dreamed of. We've all been drawn toward something we want when we know we should have walked away.

Matthew 4:1–3 describes when Jesus was tempted: "Jesus was led up by the Spirit into the wilderness to be tempted by the Devil. After He had fasted 40 days and 40 nights, He was hungry. Then the tempter approached Him and said, 'If You are the Son of God, tell these stones to become bread.'" Jesus answered Satan and faced two more challenges before the tempter left and angels came and helped Him.

Jesus was tempted with power, prestige, and wealth. Jesus was never going to succumb to these offers of the Devil, because He knew He already possessed what he offered. And He used the Word of God to remind the Devil and us that we can withstand these same assaults on our character. God knows you. He made you. He knows that you are strong enough to resist these temptations. He knows that He has placed the Word of God in your heart and that you hear His voice. We've all been tempted or asked by someone to do something we would not normally do, but we keep following Jesus and choosing His will for us. Keep following Him, Dad.

LET'S PRAY

Lord, this dad is tempted to take a path he'll regret later. His integrity is at risk, and now he wonders if he's falling into a trap of sin. He wants a good reputation, but he is struggling. You know about his disappointments in coming up short. Show him that You took the path that others would follow, and he can follow you down that path too. In Jesus' name we pray. Amen.

CONTINUE THE CONNECTION

When you face a temptation this week, consider how you can respond using the Word of God as your weapon.

46

TONIGHT WE PRAY FOR THE DAD WHO TAKES CARE OF HIS COMMUNITY

*W*hile Jesus walked the earth, He discipled and cared for His twelve friends, but not only for them. The book of Matthew provides us with a story about Jesus' compassion for those in His extended community. Matthew 15:32 records, "Jesus summoned His disciples and said, 'I have compassion on the crowd, because they've already stayed with Me three days and have nothing to eat. I don't want to send them away hungry; otherwise they might collapse on the way.'"

Jesus saw their needs and was compassionate for their obvious lack. So, calling His disciples together, He gathered seven loaves and a few fishes and multiplied them to feed four thousand men and their families. This was the second time Jesus supernaturally fed a large crowd, but this miracle was different from the previous event of loaves and fishes. At the first miracle recorded in John 6, those who gathered were on their way to a Passover feast. It was getting late in the day, and while they might have had unleavened bread with them, this food would have been reserved for the ceremonial purposes later. Jesus gave the crowd food because they likely had food but wouldn't be able to eat it. In this second event, Jesus had compassion on a crowd of four thousand who had been with Him for three days without food.

When we think of the multiplication of the bread and fish that Jesus performed, it would be easy to see them as nearly the same miracle. But Jesus saw each crowd and their circumstances as unique, and He saw the importance of meeting the needs of those around Him. As you give what you have to help your community, know that Jesus sees and appreciates your efforts.

LET'S PRAY

Lord, this dad volunteers his time, his energy, and his talents for his family and his friends. He might be a soccer coach or a youth leader. He might work as a school board member or in a food bank. He has a reputation for helping others, and those who know him are certain that he looks out for their best interests. You have multiplied his time, and You honor his acts of righteousness as unto You. Bless the work of his hands and feet. In Jesus' name we pray. Amen.

CONTINUE THE CONNECTION

How can you serve your community like Jesus this week?

47

TONIGHT WE PRAY FOR THE DAD WHO LEADS HIS FAMILY

*I*n Scripture, God didn't always choose the obvious man to lead His people. While the people chose a tall, strong King Saul, God had looked at the heart of David and chosen a man who had leadership skills that others didn't see with their eyes. The men God chooses have similar traits. They are confident in the Lord, they trust that they hear His voice, and they obediently follow Him.

Listen, Dad: you are a leader. You may or may not be a leader in other areas of your life, but you are a leader in your home. You make time for God. You pray. You seek Him when it comes to answers or direction for your family. He knows your heart, and, importantly, you know His. Throughout Scripture, good leaders knew and trusted God's heart.

Joshua 4:2–3 tells the story of men being chosen to represent their tribes: "Choose 12 men from the people, one man for each tribe, and command them: Take 12 stones from this place in the middle of the Jordan where the priests are standing, carry them with you, and set them down at the place where you spend the night." These stones were set up as a memorial of what God had done for His people—how He had safely led them, how He had been faithful to them, and how He would continue to be with them. The elders chose one man out of each tribe to pick out a stone and carry it from the Jordan to the place where an altar would be built. Each of the twelve chosen men had received the good report that they were particularly qualified to represent their family, their tribe. And just as the people would remember that God had fulfilled His promise, so also would the people remember who had been deemed worthy to complete the memorial to the Lord.

Dad, you have already been chosen by God to be a father. You have already been selected for this high calling. You don't need any additional approval. You just need to be who God already knows you are: a leader who knows God, hears His voice, and follows Him obediently.

LET'S PRAY

Lord, this dad leads his family emotionally, physically, and spiritually. He's a leader who knows Your heart. He also prays for what the family needs and leads the family in Your ways. He wants to carry them as far as he possibly can, and they see his dedication. Give him the resolve to be a leader in his home. In Jesus' name we pray. Amen.

CONTINUE THE CONNECTION

As you go about your week, remember that God chose you to be the dad to these children.

48

TONIGHT WE PRAY FOR THE DAD
WHO NEEDS HEALING

*S*cripture relates a story of Jesus' encounter with a disabled man. It is clear that Jesus did not know the man but that He learned about this man's infirmity. The suffering was obvious to Jesus, and He asked the man to tell Him more about it. The man said he had suffered a very long time, a lifetime, perhaps. He felt as though he had done everything he could do to get relief, and nothing worked. Even when he asked for help, no one was particularly concerned about him, and people ignored his pleas for assistance. They carried about their daily lives, not realizing how serious his infirmity was.

But Jesus knew exactly what the man was expressing and had compassion for him. He spoke directly to the man and asked, "Do you want to get well?" (John 5:6). When the man realized that Jesus was the healer who had healed so many in recent days, and that He might actually heal him, he wondered if healing would be possible in his circumstance. And Jesus, having compassion on him, immediately alleviated his fear and worry and pain. Jesus said to the man in

John 5:8, "Get up! Pick up your mat and walk" (NIV). And the man walked, pain free, infirmity gone, cured completely.

The Lord has the same compassion toward us that He had on this man. He may heal us in one moment, or He may heal us in other ways, just like He healed so many others throughout Scripture. The good news for us is that Jesus still heals today. Whatever you have need of, He is paying attention and desires that you would be well.

LET'S PRAY

Lord, this dad may live in pain and disability. He may have been injured on the job or suffered traumatic injury. Maybe what he faces is chronic, or it is recent. In any event, discomfort is an everyday reality for him. It certainly robs him of his peace and joy and takes away from the relationship that he would like to have with his family. But You, Lord, are his healer. You have seen his despair and his suffering. Help him know that You will fulfill Your Word to him for health and wholeness. In Jesus' name we pray. Amen.

CONTINUE THE CONNECTION

What is it that you need Jesus to do for you today? Take a moment to ask Him to touch you and heal you.

49

TONIGHT WE PRAY FOR THE DAD WHO HOLDS ON TO GOD'S PROMISES

*T*here's a story in the Bible about a young dreamer named Joseph who saved his family when famine swept through the region. Joseph is known for his coat of many colors, but his story is actually of a man who was able to trust God despite every hard circumstance and trial in order to rescue those he loved.

Genesis 37:3–5 says this:

Israel loved Joseph more than his other sons because Joseph was a son born to him in his old age, and he made a robe of many colors for him. When his brothers saw that their father loved him more than all his brothers, they hated him and could not bring themselves to speak peaceably to him. Then Joseph had a dream. When he told it to his brothers, they hated him even more.

In this dream, Joseph saw what represented his brothers bowing down to him. Full of hatred, they decided to sell Joseph into slavery.

Yet Joseph did not forget the dream. He might have been sold into slavery, but after some years he became the second in command over all of Egypt. When famine came, and Joseph's brothers traveled to find food, they bowed to Joseph, not knowing he was their brother, and asked for his help.

Joseph made the choice to help his brothers and forgive them, inviting his entire family to come live in the land of Egypt where there was more than enough for all of them. From the dream to the destiny, everything Joseph went through wasn't just for his own good, but for the good of those he loved.

Like Joseph, some of the dreams we have in our hearts aren't just for us. We might feel selfish considering the exploration of a new endeavor, wondering how it might impact our families. We must remember that when God gives us a dream, it is also for our family's benefit.

LET'S PRAY

Lord, sometimes Your dreams for this dad feel faded. But he keeps those dreams in his heart because he knows that his family believes in him. As he grows in You, give him new dreams to carry him and his family forward. Help him boldly follow You for the sake of those he loves. In Jesus' name we pray. Amen.

CONTINUE THE CONNECTION

This week as you pray, remember the dreams you've had and ask the Lord to resurrect them to your family's benefit.

50

TONIGHT WE PRAY FOR THE DAD WHO SPEAKS THE TRUTH

*A*s a dad and follower of Jesus, you recognize Truth and follow Him. The apostle Peter was just like you. He was totally committed to Jesus. He listened to what Jesus said, he watched what Jesus did. And he made sure that nothing stood in the way of Jesus doing what He said He was going to do. He also listened to the people. He knew what others said about Jesus, but after spending time with Him, Peter knew the truth, and he knew the Truth personally.

So when Jesus traveled to a region where there had been some question about His ministry and His purpose for being there, He asked His disciples what they'd heard from the people. He was testing them to see how they might respond to disputes among the people. "'But what about you?' he asked. 'Who do you say I am?' Simon Peter answered, "You are the Messiah, the Son of the living God'" (Matthew 16:15–16 NIV).

Jesus replied, "Blessed are you, Simon son of Jonah, for this was not revealed to you by flesh and blood, but by my Father in heaven.

And I tell you that you are Peter, and on this rock I will build my church, and the gates of Hades will not overcome it" (vv. 17–18 NIV).

Not a word of hesitation from Peter. The other disciples had answered with safe, politically correct responses. The truth is, based on the other disciples' answers, none of them had even considered the possibility of Peter's answer, despite all of Jesus' teaching to them. Only Peter was willing to say what he knew to be true. As a result, Jesus told Peter that not only was Peter correct in his assessment but his commitment to Jesus would remain and all of heaven would recognize it. As dads, we want to make sure that we are bold enough like Peter to say what God says is true as we follow Him and lead our children.

LET'S PRAY

Lord, when it comes down to it, this dad knows who You are. In every season, whether good or bad, even when life breaks down, he buckles down and makes sure his family knows they can count on him to speak truth into difficult situations. Just like Peter, nothing stops him. His failures don't define him. As he commits his life to You, give him courage to always know the truth and to always speak it. In Jesus' name we pray. Amen.

CONTINUE THE CONNECTION

This week, no matter what the world or your friends or those around you say, know that truth never changes and God's Word is the ultimate guide for your family.

51

TONIGHT WE PRAY FOR THE DAD WHO WONDERS IF HE CAN KEEP GOING

*M*ost of us dads live life from the middle. Not too much, not too little. We live within our means. It's enough because it has to be. You do okay in a crisis. Hailstorm, fix the roof. Sewer backup, all hands on deck. Hurricane or forest fire, safety is the number one rule.

But what if the crisis goes for days and days and days? Or years? How about if that hurricane destroyed your business or the business of the people who employed you? This isn't a crisis; this is a lifestyle change. And in situations like these, it is understandable to wonder if we are up to it.

Scripture recounts the story of a young man named Gideon living in very troubled times. Once a year, a tribe of marauders would come through the villages of his region in Israel during harvest time and totally wipe out the crops and the resources. The marauders used the villagers' crops to feed their own animals and carried the remainder off for themselves. This went on for seven years. It got so bad that the Israelites would hide their grain in the winepresses. Gideon wondered how he could keep going. In the hiding, and the working from dawn to dusk for seven years just to see everything you've worked for get carried off, you'd probably wonder too. But God saw things differently.

As Gideon was hiding with the wheat in the winepress, an angel appeared to him and said, "The LORD is with you, mighty warrior" (Judges 6:12). You see, sometimes we just have to see ourselves the way God does. You may not see yourself as any kind of warrior but just a dad who gets it done. But God sees more. By the end of the story, God encouraged Gideon, and he marshalled his people and overcame the marauders. God still sees you as a warrior who can overcome as well.

LET'S PRAY

Lord, this dad knows he can keep up with the daily trials. But sometimes a crisis comes along that really taxes him, and when the crises multiply, he can feel lost. You know his strength and You know that You made him to overcome the circumstances that seem to bury him. Remind him that he is mighty in Your sight to complete the calling You have for him, wherever it leads him. In Jesus' name we pray. Amen.

CONTINUE THE CONNECTION

Take a moment to ask the Lord to show you how He sees you. You are stronger and more capable than you realize.

52

TONIGHT WE PRAY FOR THE DAD
WHO MAKES DISCIPLES

*A*s a dad, you are familiar with the feeling of all eyes being on you. You know your children are watching you and looking up to you. You know they think of you as an example by which they will conduct themselves. It is a weighty responsibility, but you have Jesus as your example.

Scripture reminds us in John 14:26 that we have the Holy Spirit to guide us into all truth and that He will bring the Word of God to our remembrance whenever we ask. If we don't understand it, He will show us Jesus Christ in all things.

What you are is a disciple maker. You make followers of Jesus by following Him yourself. So when Scripture says in Matthew 28:19–20, "Go, therefore, and make disciples of all nations, baptizing them in the name of the Father and of the Son and of the Holy Spirit, teaching them to observe everything I have commanded you. And remember, I am with you always, to the end of the age," you understand that you live out these words daily. The word in this scripture for "go" actually means "as you are going," and it refers to how we go about our daily lives. This one word defines the entire verse, inasmuch as it focuses on our activity and who we are while we "go."

Jesus was sent to make disciples of all nations, and we are instructed to do the same—by sharing the Jesus who is already in us and sharing Him in a way that makes others want to follow Him also. When other people see what you have become, Dad, and the power and authority you have from God, Jesus says they will want to be like you, full of the Holy Spirit and truth. And as Jesus says, so it will ever be, even to the end of the age.

LET'S PRAY

Lord, there are so many ways dads can make disciples. We make disciples in Sunday school rooms, in pulpits, in life groups that meet in coffee shops or home groups that meet in our living rooms. Jesus taught on mountainsides and boats on the water. He taught while walking on the road and while having a meal. Just as it was with Jesus, there are so many places and opportunities we can share His love in our own lives. Show this dad where his opportunities for ministry can be found. In Jesus' name we pray. Amen.

CONTINUE THE CONNECTION

How are you leading your children and others
into becoming more like Jesus today?

53

TONIGHT WE PRAY FOR THE DAD WHO NEEDS A REST

$\mathcal{D}$ad, it goes without saying that you need a break. You've given it your all this week, this month, this year. You've worked really hard and you've done your best. You know there will be other responsibilities and they will come sooner rather than later, but for now, you may need a day of rest.

It's so easy to push yourself. There's always something more that can be done, right? Dad, that's not the way God sees it. He made you. He knows your strength and how much you've got left. And He also knows it's going to run out. So God wants you to plan your rest just like you plan all the other things in your life. Because if you don't, you won't.

God gives us a plan for how this looks. And you should take it seriously. There needs to be a set period of time for not working, for not always focusing on the responsibilities and things that must be done. It's a hard thing in our culture and economy, but God set it up for your good. Scripture records that He actually did these things first.

Genesis 2:1–3 reminds us, "The heavens and the earth and everything in them were completed. By the seventh day God completed His work that He had done, and He rested on the seventh day from all His work that He had done. God blessed the seventh day and declared it holy, for on it He rested from His work of creation."

He did all the necessary work in six days. What wasn't done in six days wasn't necessary. Lean into that. Schedule your time to trust that promise. On that seventh day, use it. If you like sports, do sports. If you like hiking, get outdoors. If you're a writer, write. Whatever it is that you enjoy, do it. And as you rest, remember, you aren't just relaxing from responsibilities; you are resting in the knowledge that you can trust God to make up the difference when you rest in Him.

LET'S PRAY

Lord, this dad really needs You, and he sometimes seeks permission to stop what he's doing and take a break. He knows the responsibilities continue, but he just can't get it all done all the time. Show him that You already have a plan to keep his family secure. He knows he cannot do all this by himself. The two of you are in this together. He knows it and You know it. Help him trust You with his work and his rest. In Jesus' name we pray. Amen.

CONTINUE THE CONNECTION

Take the time to intentionally rest this week. How will this show God that you trust Him?

54

TONIGHT WE PRAY FOR THE DAD WHO LOVES TO BE IN GOD'S PRESENCE

The psalmist wrote, "Better is one day in your courts than a thousand elsewhere" (Psalm 84:10 NIV). There is nothing better than the peace that comes when we are in the presence of God. Jesus would agree. When He was sent to earth to fulfill His heavenly mission of redeeming humanity back to God, He still longed to be with His Father in heaven.

There is a moment in Scripture found in Luke 2 when the young Jesus had traveled with His family to celebrate the Passover feast in Jerusalem. When the feast had concluded, His parents left with the other travelers, but they discovered after a few days that He was not with them. Searching for Him, they retraced their path back to Jerusalem, all the time wondering where He was.

When they found Him in the temple discussing the Scriptures with the elders and learned men, His mother asked what had caused Him to treat them in such a way. "'Why were you searching for Me?'

He asked them. 'Didn't you know that I had to be in My Father's house?'" (Luke 2:49).

Jesus said that He had a primary responsibility to follow His Father's leading, to do what He'd been charged to do. But it wasn't just out of obligation that He wanted to spend time at the temple. It was His love for His Father that drew Him to His house. As you commit your days to following the Lord, remember that the reward isn't just found in fulfilling your calling or obediently doing as God asks. There is joy found in simply being in God's presence, in simply being with your Father.

LET'S PRAY

Lord, just as this dad loves being with You, he understands just how much his children love to be with him. When his children call him "Dad" or "Daddy," there is nothing more precious on earth to him, because it means his children want to be in his presence. That makes his heart full. Just as You, Lord, always welcome this dad, he makes sure that his children know they are always welcome with him. His name is special and the best word on earth. Let him hear it often. In Jesus' name we pray. Amen.

CONTINUE THE CONNECTION

This week as you pray, consider the gift of simply being able to come to God and spend time with Him.

55

TONIGHT WE PRAY FOR THE DAD WHO IS IN THE MIDST OF A GREAT TRIAL

*N*one of us enjoys tests of patience or endurance. However, when we can see God's presence in trying events, it changes our character and destiny.

Many of us have heard or used the phrase "the patience of Job." This phrase relates to a scriptural account of the trials of a man who endured great calamity with little complaint. Job had much, he was well-respected, and it is likely his family would also have been blessed in equal measure. You may remember that the Lord declared in Job 1:8 that there was no one on earth like Job.

In a moment, however, all this man had—his wealth, his reputation, and his family—was taken away. He went from being great to greatly needing God. Throughout Job's suffering, he continually sought God, questioning the Lord. Finally, Scripture records, "The LORD answered Job from the whirlwind. He said: Who is this who obscures My counsel with ignorant words?" Their conversation continued, and Job eventually replied, "I had heard rumors about You, but now my eyes have seen You" (Job 38–42). Job questioned God, but he never understood that God had been present all the time, right there in the middle of the storm.

God does not give us affliction for us to become greater. He does, however, allow us to experience adversity that we can overcome with His help. And, of course, our greatest suffering occurs when we believe we are alone in our trials. While we may cry out, "Why did this happen to me?" we should instead cry, "Where are You, God?" And He will answer out of the very whirlwind of our suffering and say to us, "I was right here all along."

LET'S PRAY

Lord, there is so much more to do, and today it just seems too great for one dad to endure. He feels alone because he knows there isn't anyone who can take the physical, mental, or emotional burden off of his shoulders. But You have a plan in Your mind that will multiply his reward. Open his eyes to see where You are, and open his heart to see what greatness is in store for him when he gets to the other side of this trial. In Jesus' name we pray. Amen.

CONTINUE THE CONNECTION

Ask God to show you where He is right now
in the middle of your situation.

56

TONIGHT WE PRAY FOR THE DAD WHO TAKES CARE OF HIS PHYSICAL HEALTH

$\mathcal{D}$ad, I'm here to tell you right now that you have to take care of yourself. Now, granted, we tend to focus our time, our energies, and our talents on those most important to us: our spouse and our children. We do the things that are expected of us, and usually, these things take time. So we tend to take care of ourselves last, if at all. That's honorable, but only if we, at some point, make sure we are healthy enough to continue with those responsibilities.

First Corinthians 6:19–20 reminds us, "Don't you know that your body is a sanctuary of the Holy Spirit who is in you, whom you have from God? You are not your own, for you were bought at a price. Therefore glorify God in your body." Look at the way the apostle Paul described you. The first words here are about your body. He implied that you know about yourself and how important you are to God. So you are supposed to know how to take care of your physical health, and you should want to. When it comes down to it, God has created you so He can use you, and you need to take that responsibility seriously.

Moreover, the temple of God had implements and special adornments within it that told a story of who God was and is. Every item of furniture and golden pieces were in just the right place for just the right reason. God had declared that He would dwell in His temple. Now that you are declared to be a temple where God can also dwell, in the presence of His Holy Spirit, you must make this temple of your body a place where everything is just so. And since God has purchased you and everything you are with the price of His Son, Jesus, you should also treat what God has purchased as special.

You should not merely go about your day doing the bare minimum to take care of yourself but, rather, treat yourself with the same respect and honor with which God treats you. And listen, Dad—even if you choose to honor yourself last, you should still see yourself as God sees you, worthy of honor.

LET'S PRAY

Lord, this dad knows he needs to take care of his physical health. He knows he's important to You and valuable in Your sight. It is easy for him not to pay attention to his own health as much or as often as he should because of all the challenges of being a dad. Please remind him that he is worthy of care. And that, most of all, You want him to be healthy. In Jesus' name we pray. Amen.

CONTINUE THE CONNECTION

How can you honor God by taking care of yourself this week?

57

TONIGHT WE PRAY FOR THE
DAD WHO NEEDS FAITH

As dads, we always want to be in a position to help our children. Sometimes, despite our best efforts, we just don't know how and need to ask for help. And sometimes we don't just need practical help from others. We need God to intervene and do what only He can. Thankfully, God is already prepared for such a conversation, and He is ready, willing, and able to show us the path that leads to answers for every problem we face.

There is a story in the gospel of Mark where just such a dad arrived to ask Jesus and His disciples for help, as his son needed healing. But this dad quickly realized during the conversation with Jesus that not only did the son need healing but he himself needed to have his faith restored in God.

He said to Jesus, "'But if You can do anything, have compassion on us and help us.' Then Jesus said to him, '"If You can"? Everything is possible to the one who believes.' Immediately the father of the boy cried out, 'I do believe! Help my unbelief'" (Mark 9:22–24).

At that moment, a father realized the desperate need of his son and cried out to Jesus for help for both issues: the child's healing and his faith. You might have found yourself in a similar situation. Maybe your child does not need healing, but maybe there is another need you have brought before God, unsure if He will really meet you. Maybe like the dad in this story, you need to call out, "I do believe! Help my unbelief." Rest assured, God can change your attitude when you ask Him for guidance.

LET'S PRAY

Lord, all of us, at some time or other, have taken stock of ourselves and determined that we are not able to solve every problem in our family. We try, but we realize we need Your help. And sometimes, like the father in the story, this dad's own unbelief gets in the way of his prayers for answers. Help him as he reaches out to You, especially for the answers that seem so hard to find. You know every need he has. Please increase his faith as he trusts You more every day. In Jesus' name we pray. Amen.

CONTINUE THE CONNECTION

As you pray this week, ask: In what areas in your family life do you need increased faith? Ask the Lord to help you with any unbelief, and remember He is ready to strengthen you and meet your needs.

58

TONIGHT WE PRAY FOR THE DAD WHO THINKS HIS HANDS ARE EMPTY

*D*ad, you give it your all every day. But there are some days when you think you may have run out of resources. Maybe you've lost a job and you know how hard it can be to find another one. You may have financial problems. And then fear starts to set in. *I can take care of me all right,* you think, *but what about the kids?* And if one of them gets sick, well, that's a whole different set of circumstances. Sometimes it feels as though we are out of what we have to offer.

Scripture tells a story about a family that had used up every bit of their resources. A mother of a small child had been faithful in much as well as in little. She'd lost her husband, and the income dried up. She was prepared to use her last resources to save her child. Little did she know that God was going to use her lack of resources to do a miracle. God's plan of provision showed up in the person of Elijah, a prophet, who told her that when she completed her baking, there would be enough for all of them.

In 1 Kings 17:12–13 the widow said to Elijah,

"As the LORD your God lives, I don't have anything baked—only a handful of flour in the jar and a bit of oil in the jug. Just now, I am gathering a couple of sticks in order to go prepare it for myself and my son so we can eat it and die." Then Elijah said to her, "Don't be afraid; go and do as you have said. But first make me a small loaf from it and bring it out to me. Afterward, you may make some for yourself and your son."

Do you know what this mother did? She put her trust in God. Scripture relates that after all of them had been fed with what little they had, God replenished her entire supply of flour and oil, so that they would not starve. She believed that God would save her son. Like this woman caring for her family, your hands are not as empty as they seem. When we give the Lord what little we have, He multiplies it.

LET'S PRAY

Lord, this dad has given his all on a number of occasions. He's had more prosperous times, and he's trudged along in the scarce places. He can make it, but he wants to be faithful in what he's been given. You have a miracle for him in just these very circumstances. Help him know that since Your hands are never empty, neither will his hands be. In Jesus' name we pray. Amen.

CONTINUE THE CONNECTION

As you pray this week, trust that the Lord is sending you help.

59

TONIGHT WE PRAY FOR THE DAD WHO HAS SUFFERED GRIEF

Luke 11 tells the story about Lazarus, one of Jesus' friends. Lazarus and his two sisters, Mary and Martha, had welcomed Jesus into their home in Bethany. This had been Jesus' home base from very early on in His ministry. He had brought the disciples to this familiar place as well. Lazarus and his sisters had cared for Jesus as a family member, not just as a welcome guest. They lived together and, with the other disciples, often shared stories of the hardships and joys of Jesus' ministry. But Lazarus took ill while Jesus was away, and he died before Jesus could return.

When word was sent to Jesus that Lazarus was sick, Jesus planned when He would return to see His friend. Days later, upon His arrival, Jesus asked to see the place where Lazarus had been buried. Standing in front of the tomb, Jesus was grief-stricken. And even though the culture of the time prevented priests from approaching any tomb or shedding a tear, even for a family member, John 11:35 records, "Jesus wept."

All the people who knew Jesus realized that He must have suffered indescribably. As Jesus stood there with His family, He showed us that He truly understood loss and could experience grief as well. The same Jesus who would raise Lazarus from the dead through the power of the Holy Spirit was still moved by the realities of death. Jesus understood loss then, and He understands the pain of loss now. Whatever you are facing, you can know this: you serve a God who sympathizes with your pain and who is powerful enough to walk you through your grief. He is strong and He is sensitive, and He loves you and the person you lost just as much as He loved His friend Lazarus.

LET'S PRAY

Lord, this dad has lost a person in his life who can never be replaced. His life has been irrevocably changed. It might have been a sudden event or a life decision that caused this separation. In any event, part of his soul has been taken away. He cannot see a way through this pain. You have also experienced this dad's separation in a life of friendship and true relationship as with Your friend Lazarus. You have borne all of our sorrows and carry our griefs. Send him the true comfort today. In Jesus' name we pray. Amen.

CONTINUE THE CONNECTION

It is healing to remember that Jesus is still
saddened by grief and pain today.

60

TONIGHT WE PRAY FOR THE DAD
WHO NEEDS A NEW OUTLOOK

*W*e can all get stuck in the rut of believing what we see right in front of us is all there will ever be. *This is where I live. This is just the way my family is. This is my job, and these are the responsibilities I shoulder.* Sometimes we forget that life spent following Jesus means that in a moment God can give us fresh vision for our future.

A story in Mark 10:49–52 of a blind man named Bartimaeus reminds us that this is true. His disability required that he stay separate and apart from people, but he received money by begging from a remote location. And as people would pass by, the culture required them to give alms to him. So Bartimaeus depended on the generosity of others. He could not provide for himself, and he had no hope or expectation for any future. The way it was for Bartimaeus was the way it always would be.

So when he heard the commotion of a great crowd, and having heard from those who had passed by in recent days that the Messiah had arrived, he begged in a loud voice to be able to reach Jesus, who was walking by. Mark records, "Jesus stopped and said, 'Call him.' So they called the blind man and said to him, 'Have courage! Get up; He's calling for you.' He threw off his coat, jumped up, and came to Jesus" (10:49–50). When he reached Jesus, He asked Bartimaeus what he wanted Jesus to do for him. Bartimaeus said he wanted to see. Jesus told him that his faith had healed him, and in that moment Bartimaeus received his sight and began following Jesus.

Note that when Jesus told him to come, he threw off his coat—a coat that would identify him as blind—and went to Jesus. Bartimaeus followed Jesus into a brand-new life from that day forward. We must never forget that when we encounter Jesus, we are given the same hope of fresh vision just like Bartimaeus was.

LET'S PRAY

Lord, we pray for the dad who needs a new vision. He's been toiling for some time now, and he's had some successes. But he doesn't want to settle for enough. He believes he's capable of even more, and he wants to provide in a new and better way. He's taken care of his family by watching and praying. Lord, this dad believes You bless us. Open his eyes to clearly see the path You've chosen for him to walk in. In Jesus' name we pray. Amen.

CONTINUE THE CONNECTION

This week, ask the Lord to give you fresh sight so
you can follow Him into new adventures.

61

TONIGHT WE PRAY FOR THE DAD WHO WORSHIPS

*S*econd Samuel 6:13–15 records a story about King David. When David was king, he discovered that God had blessed the household of Obed-edom because the ark of God was there with them. The ark was a sacred box covered in gold that held important artifacts, including the tables of the Ten Commandments. This wasn't just any ordinary ark; it represented God's presence. So David had the ark brought to his city with great joy: "Wearing a linen ephod, David was dancing before the LORD with all his might, while he and all Israel were bringing up the ark of the LORD with shouts and the sound of trumpets" (NIV).

When King David brought the ark of God, which represents God's presence, back to the city of David, he rejoiced. It was as though God Himself was coming back into the city. David didn't just dance and worship; he was undignified in his show of love. Scripture explains that David danced with all his might. Why? The full history of this passage reminds us that David recognized who God was and that God's promises were coming to pass. In response, he danced and he sang and he feasted. David realized that wherever the ark of God was, there would be peace and provision and rest because God was present. David's joy for being near the ark of God overwhelmed him. He couldn't help but worship.

When you stop to think about it, God has done many marvelous things in your life too. There are things you've prayed for and things that were unexpected, when God performed a mighty work on your behalf. Didn't you feel like rejoicing? When you are in God's presence, He wants you to dance and sing. (Not as a requirement, but because of the joy it represents.) He wants you to have joy. He wants you to remember that He has done many things for you and that there are more coming.

LET'S PRAY

Lord, this dad loves to be in Your presence. He has joy and peace in everything You are to him. He knows that when he is in Your presence, everything is wonderful and all will be well. Just like a small child in his father's arms, this dad knows that You have everything under control. He worships because he knows Your promises come to pass and that he need never fear. Bless him continually, as only a father can. In Jesus' name we pray. Amen.

CONTINUE THE CONNECTION

When was the last time you celebrated what God has done in your life? Take time this week to praise!

62

TONIGHT WE PRAY FOR THE
DAD WHO NEEDS HELP

*A*s you likely know, Jesus, who was often questioned, rarely spoke direct answers. Instead, He offered parables, giving the hearer an opportunity to discern their own interpretation. In Luke 10:29, Jesus was asked the question, "Who is my neighbor?" He responded with the story found in Luke 10:30–37.

"A man was going down from Jerusalem to Jericho and fell into the hands of robbers. They stripped him, beat him up, and fled, leaving him half dead." Jesus went on to say that two men passed by, not wanting to be of any assistance. But then, an unlikely hero came upon this man left for dead and took him to a place of rest and provision.

Many of Jesus' parables are lessons contained within a story. We often talk about being the neighbor who stopped to help, but what happens should you relate more to the man who was taking a journey and, suddenly through no fault of his own, was robbed of everything he possessed? In this story, this traveler was probably a regular man going about his everyday life. In the custom of the time he probably had all or most of his belongings with him as he traveled. Therefore, when he was robbed, everything was taken. I wonder if you can relate to him. Bad things happen to us through no fault of our own, such as natural disasters, a global pandemic, and business failure. The hope for us in this story is that God will always send us help—and sometimes this help will take unexpected forms.

It often happens that the people you think should come to your aid do not, and sometimes God uses a person or a process we wouldn't have first considered to bring the restoration we need. Whether you're the man who has suffered loss or you're the man who can stop to help, know this: God has not forgotten about you. Help is on the way.

LET'S PRAY

Lord, this dad needs Your help. Whatever the cause of his loss, whatever he needs You to restore, he feels discouraged and he doesn't know where to turn. He's worried about how he's going to take care of his family. Remind him that You will not leave him forsaken and You will send the help he needs. Give him that assurance daily. In Jesus' name we pray. Amen.

CONTINUE THE CONNECTION

This week as you pray, ask God to show you from
what unexpected places help might come.

63

TONIGHT WE PRAY FOR THE DAD
WHO RUNS TO THE LORD

*D*ad, where did you last leave Jesus? Were the two of you together facing an uncertain future when He provided the answer to the puzzle of your life and you ran off to tell everybody that you figured it out? Or had you just received a promotion in your career, with the upshot that everything was going to work out better than you had imagined, and you told Him, "I guess I'll take it from here"?

Scripture relates the story of Jesus' resurrection from the tomb on Sunday morning. Peter and John (who referred to himself as "the other disciple") had heard from Mary Magdalene that the tomb, where all of the disciples expected Him to be, was empty. They had seen Him perish and they had seen Him properly placed in a tomb. That was it. That was where they left Him. And that's where they expected Him to be.

So when they heard He wasn't in the tomb anymore, they ran to where they had last seen Him. John 20:3–4 says, "At that, Peter and the other disciple went out, heading for the tomb. The two were running together, but the other disciple outran Peter and got to the tomb first." Dad, they ran. The moon had set, the sun had not come up, and it was dark. And they ran. They ran because they still didn't believe that He might actually have risen from that tomb. Or they ran because they were overjoyed that they wouldn't be alone after all. Or they ran because they thought maybe He might have been alive and they could speak with Him again and go on as they had together.

Suddenly, He was the answer again. John arrived first, but Scripture says that when Peter reached the tomb he went right in. He wanted to know on his own terms that Jesus was who He said He was. Nothing and no one would keep Peter out. Dad, these men ran for all the reasons you might. You may run to Him when you doubt. You may run to Him when you need to know He's still with you. You may run to Him when you know He will help you through your difficulties. But you always run, and Jesus is always glad to meet you again.

LET'S PRAY

Lord, this dad needs You. You're there in the bright of day, and You're there in the dark of night. This dad always wants to know that You hear his prayers. And he runs to You in each and every circumstance. Remind him that You have an answer to every question he has and that You will always be beside him. In Jesus' name we pray. Amen.

CONTINUE THE CONNECTION

When was the last time you ran to Jesus for what you needed?

64

TONIGHT WE PRAY FOR THE DAD WHO HAS LOST HIS FAITH

*W*e all go through seasons when we don't see, hear, or perceive God as clearly. We may doubt His plan or lose hope in our ability to follow His leading.

Scripture relates a story where the disciples had gathered after the resurrection of Jesus to share their thoughts and feelings about what a life without Jesus might mean. Thomas, who had been a faithful disciple and always wanted to go with Jesus and follow Him wherever He went, happened to be out of the room for this conversation. It was then that Jesus appeared and encouraged His friends.

Upon Thomas's return, the disciples eagerly shared the good news, telling Thomas that Jesus had risen from the dead. Thomas's response? "If I don't see the mark of the nails in His hands, put my finger into the mark of the nails, and put my hand into His side, I will never believe!" (John 20:25).

Thomas had been a man of great faith, once even saying that if Jesus were to die, he would go with Him. On another occasion he had asked Jesus to tell him exactly how He planned to go and prepare a house, wondering if they could come too. But something happened to Thomas after Jesus had been crucified and buried. Thomas was lost, his life's purpose taken away. Even when his closest friends told him that Jesus was alive, and they knew not just by hearing but by seeing, Thomas had already decided that his life was irrevocably changed. But Jesus knew Thomas and just how close Thomas's heart was to His own. He knew what Thomas had said he needed to believe for himself. So when the disciples had gathered together again, Jesus came and proved Himself to this doubting friend. And Thomas's faith was restored.

Jesus gives us another chance to believe as well. You aren't the doubter. You are a friend who needs to be reminded who God is and who you are.

LET'S PRAY

Lord, this dad was strong in his confidence that everything would work out as he had planned. He believed that he and his family were on a path to peace and comfort in their home. But events have conspired to cause him to doubt. You can help him regain his confidence, peace, and assurance once again. Prove Yourself once again in his life. In Jesus' name we pray. Amen.

CONTINUE THE CONNECTION

Take a moment to pray and ask the Lord to renew your faith. He knows what your heart needs, and He is willing to meet with you.

65

TONIGHT WE PRAY FOR THE DAD WHO HAS A DAY THAT SPILLS INTO NIGHT

I'm fairly certain that you have had a sleepless night or two. Probably all dads do. The life you live in the day probably spills over into the sleeping hours occasionally, if not often. You've also probably noticed that nothing gets fixed just by staying awake. God has it in His mind that there will be a time when you will be asleep and, trust me, He's good with it. You should know that God can use a fully rested dad much better than a dad who has worried, not worked, himself to exhaustion.

The psalmist wrote in Psalm 4:8, "I will both lie down and sleep in peace, for You alone, LORD, make me live in safety." The psalmist declared as a confirmation to God that he was going to take God at His Word. He would lie down, which means that he would no longer consider the affairs of the day. And even more importantly, he would allow sleep to refresh his body and his mind.

You probably prepare your day with planning and expectation. You know there are only so many hours in this day and the have-tos are so, so important. And because some of the have-tos are our responsibility, we worry and fret over what didn't get done. You're a dad who does his best. And, at the end of the day, you need to believe you did just that. God says that as you trust in Him, you are entitled to sweet sleep (Proverbs 3:24). But still, what about those extra hours tossing and turning? What should you do? The psalmist said that you have to trust God. He said that only God can make you live in safety. God continues to make you live in safety when you are asleep. So when you awake with the problems of yesterday in your head, thank God for the promise of tomorrow. And when you arise, you will remember that His mercy, His provision of everything we need—including answers to tough questions—is all new every morning.

LET'S PRAY

Lord, this dad knows that rest can be in short supply these days, but he believes that You will provide for him even as he rests. Remind him that You always have his back, even when he sleeps. Multiply the results of his sleep tonight, and give him peace about the days ahead. In Jesus' name we pray. Amen.

CONTINUE THE CONNECTION

Do you prioritize sleep? This week, think about the Lord being involved in even your sleeping hours. Invite Him to give you peace.

66

TONIGHT WE PRAY FOR THE DAD WHO WANTS TO SET A GOOD EXAMPLE FOR HIS CHILDREN

*W*hen Jesus walked the earth, He did many things. He taught. He healed. He delivered people from spiritual bondage. He revealed truth. Ultimately He went to the cross, where He died as a sacrifice on our behalf. He rose from the dead and broke the power of sin, hell, and the grave. He did so much. Yet for every step He took, every word He spoke, and every life He influenced, He wasn't on His own. Everything Jesus did was a reflection of His heavenly Father.

When He was talking with His friends one day, He said, "I assure you: The Son is not able to do anything on His own, but only what He sees the Father doing. For whatever the Father does, the Son also does these things in the same way" (John 5:19). Up until that point, many knew what God wanted them to do, but they hadn't seen it lived out. And the disciples certainly did not understand a relationship with God apart from the teachings of the Scriptures or the teachings of the priests and rabbis. This was astonishing to them; that they could treat

God as though He was physically present. Jesus revealed His Father in heaven.

Once Christ came, the disciples had an example to follow. The good news for us is that through Jesus we, too, have a living example of what it means to be a son and what it means to be a father.

LET'S PRAY

Lord, this dad wants to be a good example for his children. He doesn't shirk responsibilities just because he works hard or away from home. He is present in the lives of his children. He manages the needs of scraped knees and hurt feelings as well as the oil changes and water heaters. He is practical and he is personal. His sons and daughters take notice of his hard work and goodness to the people in their lives. He is better each day because his kids are watching. You set the ultimate example. He just has to follow You. Bless him tonight with even more wisdom and strength. In Jesus' name we pray. Amen.

CONTINUE THE CONNECTION

This week as you pray, ask the Lord to show you any area in your life that needs to be strengthened so that you might be a better example to your children. Then ask for His help to do just that.

67

TONIGHT WE PRAY FOR THE DAD WHO EXPECTS GOD TO INTERVENE IN HIS DAILY LIFE

*I*f you're like me, you probably make plans because you expect them to come to pass. However, sometimes we get so caught up in our own plans that we don't allow the presence of God to move in our lives in an unexpected way. Sometimes, after going to church, we might totally leave God out of our week, and then we're surprised when He intervenes in our daily life. But this is what we should expect. Because often this intervention leads to a greater opportunity. As God becomes more a part of our daily lives, we should not only expect these interruptions but also anticipate them with great joy.

Many times in Scripture the Lord intervenes in the lives of His children and causes a change of plans. One such event happened to the apostle Paul. Paul was making plans to go to an area where he was well known and respected. But while making those plans, he had a vision of a man from Macedonia, which at that time was the gateway to Europe. Scripture says, "A vision appeared to Paul in the night. A man of Macedonia stood and pleaded with him, saying, 'Come over to Macedonia and help us.' Now after he had seen the vision, immediately we sought to go to Macedonia, concluding that the Lord had called us to preach the gospel to them" (Acts 16:9–10 NKJV).

Dad, just as God interrupted Paul's plans to do something he was familiar with and comfortable with, He will sometimes interrupt our weeks with His assignments. You might feel led to help a neighbor, pause to spend intentional time with your kids, or serve in some capacity you hadn't anticipated. The good news is that when this happens, it is often a gateway to something great.

LET'S PRAY

Lord, this dad trusts You, and while he makes plans, he knows that sometimes You change them. Should he doubt in Your timing, remind him that You are still in charge of times and dates. Remind him that You see him where he is and where he is going to be, and You have great adventures for him when he pauses to follow you. In Jesus' name we pray. Amen.

CONTINUE THE CONNECTION

Can you remember a time when the Lord interrupted your week and set you on another path? Think about that during your prayer time and ask Him to do it again.

68

TONIGHT WE PRAY FOR THE DAD WHO GETS TO TRY AGAIN

*W*e have all made mistakes, gotten it wrong, and had to turn around and say that we need to try again. When it comes to our relationship with the Lord, the good news is He always gives us the chance to keep going and not get stuck in what we might consider failures.

In John 21, we read a story about Peter. Peter did what many of us might consider the unthinkable. He denied that he'd ever known Jesus. Peter knew the truth, but when Jesus was going to the cross, Peter disavowed who Jesus was and, in so doing, his own destiny as one who would continue His work.

It's natural to think that after this event, in Peter's mind at least, he was damaged goods and certainly of no earthly or heavenly use to Jesus. But after Jesus rose from the dead, they met again on a beach and all was restored. While the disciples were out fishing, Jesus called to them from shore. John 21:7 says, "Now when Simon Peter heard that it was the Lord, he put on his outer garment (for he had removed it), and plunged into the sea" (NKJV). Peter was bold enough to look Jesus in

His eyes and tell Him he remembered what He had asked him to do, and that if given another chance, he would do it well.

Every day we have the same opportunity. Whether you feel near to Jesus or far from shore, He calls to us all and says, "Will you keep following Me? Will you keep taking care of My sheep?" As a dad, each day you get to decide.

LET'S PRAY

Lord, this dad has had trials and setbacks—that's for sure. After a while, he might see himself as flawed in some manner because he just can't get out of his own way. And suddenly it's no longer about just making a mistake here and there. He begins to think he is flawed, and his mistakes become attacks on his attitude and destiny. Lord, help him look for You on the "beaches" of his life and be ready to swim for his destiny. Help him keep his spiritual eyes forward to see what lies ahead. In Jesus' name we pray. Amen.

CONTINUE THE CONNECTION

This week in prayer, take time to acknowledge that you have made mistakes and to simply repent, which means to turn around. In other words, turn around and swim for the beach to find Jesus.

69

TONIGHT WE PRAY FOR THE DAD WHO UNDERSTANDS THE POWER OF COMMUNION

*I*n 1 Corinthians 11:23–26, the apostle Paul related the story of the Last Supper between Jesus and His disciples.

> The Lord Jesus took bread, gave thanks, broke it, and said, "This is My body, which is for you. Do this in remembrance of Me." In the same way, after supper He also took the cup and said, "This cup is the new covenant established by My blood. Do this, as often as you drink it, in remembrance of Me." For as often as you eat this bread and drink the cup, you proclaim the Lord's death until He comes.

When we think of this Communion meal, we remember what Jesus did on the cross; but for these men, this meal was the last time they sat with Jesus before He was crucified. There had been laughter and joy in the three or so years they had traveled and been together. They'd seen miracles. They'd survived catastrophic storms, persecution, and violence. And they'd done it all together. So on that night, with everyone gathered as we might for our holidays, they ate together. They were family. Jesus and His disciples loved each other. And this meal wasn't just a marker of what would come, but a time in remembrance of all they had been through together.

Dad, when some leader offers the elements of Communion, remember the words of Jesus quoted by Paul: "Do this in remembrance of Me." Paul reminds us that acting in remembrance is not merely remembering what someone told you, or what you read in a book. It is eating bread and drinking wine as though you were really there. With Jesus. Experiencing Jesus. On the other side of the cross. Don't just remember His death. Like His friends, remember His life. There is power in communing with King Jesus, your Friend.

LET'S PRAY

Lord, this dad knows that Jesus Christ came to save him. He always wants to better understand the power of a relationship with the risen Christ. Help him experience the presence of Jesus when he shares Communion in his community. In Jesus' name we pray. Amen.

CONTINUE THE CONNECTION

Like the disciples of Jesus, you have had your own adventures with Him. Pause to remember what you and the Lord have been through together.

70

TONIGHT WE PRAY FOR THE DAD
WHO IS RUNNING ON EMPTY

*Y*ou know those days that are so long they feel like a week's worth of trouble can be found in them? We all do. We have all experienced times when the sun goes down at the end of the day and we finally sleep, but we only find our physical rest restored. We still need a reprieve in our souls from thoughts of desperation. We still need hope in a big way.

In Psalm 27:13–14, David, the psalmist, wrote, "I am certain that I will see the LORD's goodness in the land of the living. Wait for the LORD; be strong and courageous." David was no stranger to the onslaught of enemy attack. In the rest of this psalm, he spoke of having a host of warriors encamped about him, hoping to catch him unawares, hoping that his preparation would fail him and that he would be suddenly defeated. In those times when David had nothing left, when his flesh was used up, when his mind could not come up with a plan, when his spirit had no joy or strength, David said that he would see the goodness of the Lord while he was alive, that tomorrow would be the fulfillment of God's plan for today. He knew that even when it seemed like God wasn't coming to defeat the army surrounding him, He was.

King David, despite his wisdom and strength and assurance that God was with him, still often experienced fear and trepidation. Maybe you feel the same way. Maybe despite God's blessings and provision, you experience times of fear, times of trouble, times when it seems certain that the entire world is chasing you down a blind path. David remained confident, and we can as well. We can cry out to God in those times and, once again, experience the goodness of the Lord. As He calms our fears and steadies our determination, desperation lifts. It's even better than a good night of sleep. The sense of peace and security found in God's constant presence comes over us and reminds us that we can move ahead another day. Always, always, always wait for the Lord.

LET'S PRAY

Lord, this dad believes he has to give it his best effort even when he is running on empty. Being a dad is hard work, and he needs to know that he can make it through the day. This dad needs courage to go with his determination. Strengthen him so his family will know that they can count on him. In Jesus' name we pray. Amen.

CONTINUE THE CONNECTION

Like David, make a point to confess daily what you expect to see God do for you.

71

TONIGHT WE PRAY FOR THE DAD WHO DESERVES RECOGNITION

*M*any dads do not have too many opportunities to feel special, important, or unique in their daily lives. There are birthdays and anniversaries, of course, which merely mark the passage of time. Sometimes there are promotions and graduations. But rarely do we get to have a sense of importance or recognition. However, God understands your value to Him as His son.

An important moment took place in Jesus' life when His heavenly Father recognized Him in front of a crowd. A prominent religious leader, John the Baptist, was baptizing followers, and Jesus of Nazareth asked if He could be baptized as well. Jesus, the Son of God, asked if He could experience the same blessing as all of those who were present. Not only was this something He wanted to do, He chose to do this because His own Father had asked Him to do it. It was to fulfill a calling set on His life from the beginning of time. As Jesus was dipped into the water and then pulled up again, Matthew 3:17 records, "There came a voice from heaven: 'This is My beloved Son. I take delight in

Him!'" Jesus was beloved before that moment, and in everything that followed, those who saw this event knew that Jesus would continue to be loved by His Father.

Dad, you are that son. Like Jesus, you are beloved by the Father. Before you ever entered the scene of this particular life, you were special to God. There may not be a voice from heaven causing people to stop and take notice whenever you enter a room, but you have a special place in God's heart that no one else can fill. Just as you may have more than one child but each of them has a unique place in your heart. You may not receive recognition for all you do, but God recognizes you as His son. And He is pleased.

LET'S PRAY

Lord, this dad knows that tomorrow his family's needs will continue and that he will continue to meet them with or without recognition. There will be bills to pay and peace to make in his home. As always, he will have to see further, walk faster, and prepare better than yesterday. But remind him that You are already well pleased with him as tomorrow comes. Give him confidence that he is Your beloved son. In Jesus' name we pray. Amen.

CONTINUE THE CONNECTION

This week as you pray, think about the special days in your own life and the ways in which the Lord blessed you on those days with the love of your family.

72

TONIGHT WE PRAY FOR THE DAD WHO IS GRATEFUL FOR BROTHERS HE CAN COUNT ON

*F*amily is everything. They can be the greatest asset we have. They are usually our closest allies and dearest friends. If you grew up with brothers and sisters, you probably spent more time with them than any other children. They know your stories, your strengths, and your weaknesses. If you have a friend who is close like a brother, you know you can count on him to come through for you when you need him most.

Scripture tells us a story of two brothers. One considered himself slow of speech, perhaps because he had been in the wilderness tending sheep for the last forty years and had spent those years conversing almost exclusively with God. The other was a highly skilled speaker in front of important men. God decided to use the strengths of each brother to set the children of Israel free from Egyptian slavery. In so doing, the two came to rely on each other.

Together these brothers, Moses and Aaron, were to convince Pharaoh to release the children of Israel from the bondage they were under. And they were going to have to convince the people that God sent them. When God first called Moses to this task, Moses expressed his concern, wondering how he could take on this responsibility on his own. God answered in Exodus 4:14–15: "He said, 'Isn't Aaron the Levite your brother? I know that he can speak well. And also, he is on his way now to meet you. He will rejoice when he sees you. You will speak with him and tell him what to say. I will help both you and him to speak and will teach you both what to do.'"

Dad, Jesus set you on a path and has given you instructions on how to live your life and how to live in fulfillment of everything He has for you. And He sent His Holy Spirit as a Guide, as a Counselor, as One who Scripture says walks closer than a brother (Proverbs 18:24). You likely have men in your life who are like brothers to you, but you also have the Holy Spirit. Together, you can face anything.

LET'S PRAY

Lord, this dad is grateful for the brothers You have given him. He is also grateful for Your Holy Spirit. He remembers the joys and sorrows experienced together. Moses and Aaron weren't perfect, but they had a job to do together for You. This dad believes that his brother is a gift, and he is grateful for the friend he can count on. Bless them both. In Jesus' name we pray. Amen.

CONTINUE THE CONNECTION

Take some time in prayer to thank God for the brothers in your life.

73

TONIGHT WE PRAY FOR THE
DAD WHO CAN CHANGE

$\mathcal{D}$ad, if you've lived very long, you probably have a certain way you do things. Whether you work outside or inside of the home, you likely have a daily routine. A routine helps us cope in stressful times. But sometimes the routine actually gets in the way of our family's growth and relationships. If we're not careful, we will overlook subtle changes, especially with our children. And if we miss these changes, we have missed them forever because we were busy being comfortable in our routine.

Scripture reports in John's gospel that Jesus and His disciples were together for a feast. Here, Jesus was the host and everything was set up for Him to be honored. But then, "He got up from supper, laid aside His robe, took a towel, and tied it around Himself. Next, He poured water into a basin and began to wash His disciples' feet and to dry them with the towel tied around Him" (John 13:4–5).

You can probably assume that these were not the actions of a host, of the guest of honor. In that culture, for that evening, at that dinner, this was a monumental change in behavior, and Jesus was doing it. Jesus had noticed at this dinner, after the eating, that there had been some strife. The disciples had argued about who was the most important and who should sit in a place of honor next to Jesus. So He removed His garments of importance and He focused on the disciples in the manner of the day that would show them honor and respect. He stooped and washed their feet.

Dad, it's easy to get caught up in our own responsibilities and become inflexible. But there are other important lives in your family, and you should always be mindful of who needs you to be ready to adjust when necessary. It's important to take the time to change your way of doing things so that you don't miss milestones and the accomplishments as well as the joys and the tears.

LET'S PRAY

Lord, this dad loves his children. And he tries to provide for them in every way possible. But he needs to keep his eyes and ears open to the changes that happen every day. You have shown him that if he takes a moment to listen, he can have even more peace. Help him make the changes necessary that will keep his family strong. In Jesus' name we pray. Amen.

CONTINUE THE CONNECTION

In what areas could you be more flexible?

74

TONIGHT WE PRAY FOR THE DAD WHO NEEDS TO FORGIVE

*E*phesians 4:32 says, "Be kind and compassionate to one another, forgiving one another, just as God also forgave you in Christ." In Paul's letter to the Ephesians, as with most of his writing, he expressed the belief that following after Jesus is always a continuous action. By that I mean, when we follow Jesus, it is a daily event. We aren't just supposed to be kind occasionally. We are supposed to be continually kind. We are supposed to be continually tenderhearted. And here, most importantly, we are supposed to be continually forgiving of one another.

When Paul spoke of forgiving, he likened it to what Jesus did and does for us. We are forgiven continually. We are supposed to be in a continual attitude of forgiveness in exactly the same manner as Jesus is with us. Even as He forgave us for each sin, He forgave us of all our sins. Just as there was no crime that would prevent Jesus from forgiving you, so also must it be that no offense against you is so big that it cannot be forgiven.

Listen, Dad—Jesus knows that when we hold grudges, or withhold forgiveness, we bind ourselves up with the hurts of the offenses. Meanwhile, the offender doesn't suffer the way we do. Often they don't know what they've done. We want them to be sorry, and they're just not. Our unforgiveness is as if we wait in a prison cell for them to apologize so we can be free, but the door is locked *from the inside.* When we use the key of forgiveness that is in our own hands, we can unlock that prison door and walk out into freedom. Your freedom is worth the work to forgive.

LET'S PRAY

Lord, this dad's been offended—and that's putting it mildly. There have been instances when he's been hurt or betrayed by people he trusted. He hates how this makes him feel inside, and he wonders how trust will ever be restored—or if he even wants to restore it. You saved us and reminded us that we needed much forgiving. Show this dad that his best answer is to forgive like You did. In the meantime, keep him safe in Your peace as he looks to become a better dad. In Jesus' name we pray. Amen.

CONTINUE THE CONNECTION

Make the bold choice in the next few days to use the key of forgiveness in your hands to free yourself from the prison of pain.

75

TONIGHT WE PRAY FOR THE DAD WHO IS OVERWHELMED WITH LIFE

Jesus had spent a day teaching the multitudes, expounding on the Scriptures, and showing them about the kingdom of heaven in stories. The people would have had Him stay longer, but the day was ending. He told the disciples that since He was tired, they should all retire to a different side of the Sea of Galilee. The sea was surrounded by low mountains; weather could change abruptly and often did. This day was no different. Once the boat with Jesus and the disciples had gone about halfway across the sea, a storm arose that was so strong, the disciples were afraid the boat might sink. Mark 4:37 records, "A fierce windstorm arose, and the waves were breaking over the boat, so that the boat was already being swamped." The disciples were afraid.

Remember, these were accomplished fishermen who had seen such storms before. But this one scared them to the point that they felt it necessary to warn Jesus of the danger. Scripture continues, "But He was in the stern, sleeping on the cushion. So they woke Him up and said to Him, 'Teacher! Don't You care that we're going to die?' He got up, rebuked the wind, and said to the sea, 'Silence! Be still!' The wind ceased, and there was a great calm" (vv. 38–39).

The disciples were terrified, but no amount of their panicked pleading would cause Jesus to become alarmed. There wasn't anything they could say or feel that would change His attitude toward the situation or their fear. You may feel like these men. You understand how severe storms like the one you're in can be. But, Dad, Jesus is still in your boat—and just as He confronted the storm, the subject of the disciples' fears, and supernaturally caused the sea and the wind to return to their natural state, so also can He take authority of all your fears and bring you into the place where you are at peace.

LET'S PRAY

Lord, this dad is afraid. All the circumstances of his life have become what feels like a massive storm, and he's not sure just how he's going to get across the sea. He's dealt with trials as they have come, but now, today, he's not sure he can manage. And there doesn't appear to be any relief in sight. This dad's confidence in You can help him overcome each and every obstacle he faces. Show him how to get through each day and calm his fears for tomorrow. In Jesus' name we pray. Amen.

CONTINUE THE CONNECTION

Take a moment to ask God to calm your fear and
bring peace to the situations you're facing.

76

TONIGHT WE PRAY FOR THE DAD
WHO GOES ABOVE AND BEYOND

*W*e have talked at some length about our guy Peter. We've talked about how Peter recognized when there was an opportunity to set things right with Jesus and swam to the shore. When Peter first met Jesus, he was fishing. Jesus told him to throw his net to the other side, and supernaturally Peter caught so many fish it almost sank the boat (Luke 5:5). When Peter was restored, the same thing happened. The disciples were fishing, and Jesus called to them from the shore and they supernaturally caught an abundance of fish when they followed His commands to try the net on the other side (John 21:6).

Peter was so eager to reach Jesus and reconcile their relationship that he left his fish and swam to Jesus. The disciples towed the net of fish to the beach, and after Peter and Jesus talked, Jesus told him in John 21:10, "Bring some of the fish which you have just caught" (NKJV).

Then Peter singlehandedly pulled a net full of fish on the shore to Jesus, a net so full it usually took many men to accomplish the task.

Peter remembered who he really was, as a fisherman and a fisher of men. And the moment he remembered, a supernatural strength came over him. Jesus might have said to bring a few fish, but Peter brought the whole catch. As He did with Peter, when God calls us to something, He supernaturally strengthens us to accomplish it. That's who you really are. You're the dad who goes above and beyond, because you know the One who calls you to accomplish His work is faithful.

LET'S PRAY

Lord, this dad is up for any challenge. You see, children are watching, and he shows them every day how to have a good work ethic. They give maximum effort because he does, and he wants them to know how to give God their all. He wants them to never give up when it's hard, because they know who strengthens them. He wants them to know that they can finish what they start. Bless him. In Jesus' name we pray. Amen.

CONTINUE THE CONNECTION

This week, as you face whatever challenges may come, remember God will equip you with the strength to follow His leading.

77

TONIGHT WE PRAY FOR THE DAD WHO NEEDS A FRIEND HE CAN TRUST

*T*he mutual ministry of Paul and Silas as partners in the Lord encourages us as dads to have a close friend to rely on. Paul believed that he and Silas were especially well equipped to reach non-Jewish believers together because they had a lot in common in their own individual lives, even though their ministry styles and opportunities had started out differently. They did not begin together, but they forged a relationship together, encouraging each other whenever there were difficulties. When Paul and Silas called out a false prophet for defrauding the people, the authorities, who had been a part of this fraud, had them beaten and thrown into prison. Yet the duo never stopped praising God.

Acts 16:23–26 says this:

When they had laid many stripes upon them, they cast them into prison, charging the jailor to keep them safely: Who, having received such a charge, thrust them into the inner prison, and made their feet fast in the stocks. And at midnight Paul and Silas prayed, and sang praises unto God: and the prisoners heard them. And suddenly there was a great earthquake, so that the foundations of the prison were shaken: and immediately all the doors were opened, and every one's bands were loosed. (KJV)

They traveled together, they were beaten together, and they worshipped together. They also went forth together.

Dad, Scripture shows how there is strength in friendship in good times and bad. Even if you come from different backgrounds, the Lord will bring people into your life to walk alongside you for a purpose. Let's remember the importance of cultivating friendships this week.

LET'S PRAY

Lord, this dad needs someone who will keep him looking to You. He needs a person who will encourage him and work with him daily to accomplish his best. No man can do everything alone. Our daily walk needs to be as it was with Paul and Silas, following You in the easy times as well as the difficult times. Bless this dad as he commits himself anew to growing in friendship. In Jesus' name we pray. Amen.

CONTINUE THE CONNECTION

Take time to reach out to friends this week.

78

TONIGHT WE PRAY FOR THE DAD WHO KNOWS HE HAS A PURPOSE AND A DESTINY

A dad who lives in a world of purpose and destiny will always have more than enough. He anticipates success in whatever God has tasked him with. He doesn't even consider the possibility that he might fail. He arises with hope, with conviction, and with the promise of God for his family. He believes God's words spoken through the prophet, Jeremiah, when He said, "I know the plans I have for you. . . . They are plans for good and not for disaster, to give you a future and a hope" (Jeremiah 29:11 NLT). Success should not be an abstract thought to a dad. Why? Because God promises good plans for hope and not disaster.

Isn't this what you want? To know that when you arise from sleep, your heavenly Father has already been working on your behalf toward His expected end? To know that He prepares the way for each of us?

Jeremiah went on to share God's words for us, saying, "When you pray, I will listen. If you look for me wholeheartedly, you will find me. I will be found by you" (vv. 12–14 NLT). Purpose and destiny arise in our hearts from a realization that God is present in our lives and that anything is possible. And that realization is achieved by calling on Him at every opportunity and experiencing His goodness to respond.

So, Dad, your heavenly Father anticipates that you will call on Him. He expects you to look to Him for direction. In Him you will find your purpose. In Him you will find your destiny.

LET'S PRAY

Lord, remind this dad that You are and always have been with him at every step. He knows that just as a child in his dad's arms expects everything to work out and he has nothing to fear, this dad also knows he has nothing to fear. He can trust the promise of his heavenly Father. He knows You have good plans for him. He knows You hear him. And he knows that his destiny is found as he looks to You. In this, he will find success. Let him feel Your presence even more tomorrow. In Jesus' name we pray. Amen.

CONTINUE THE CONNECTION

This week as you pray, consider what you need God to help with in order to be successful. Remember, He hears your prayers when you call to Him.

79

TONIGHT WE PRAY FOR THE DAD WHO KNOWS THAT HE HAS THE MIND OF CHRIST

$\mathcal{D}$ad, we have discussed at some length the battles we face as fathers. We go to battle for our families daily, always striving to be better. There is, however, one battle we have yet to address—the battle of our thoughts.

Paul wrote to the Roman church, "Do not conform to the pattern of this world, but be transformed by the renewing of your mind. Then you will be able to test and approve what God's will is—his good, pleasing and perfect will" (Romans 12:2 NIV). This idea of renewing your mind is a continual action. Paul didn't say "renew once." We don't renew our thoughts when we become followers of Christ and live with a perfect mind from that moment forward. Our current state as humans requires us to be continually renewing our minds.

Dad, this battle may seem hard, but 1 Corinthians 2:16 reminds you, "We have the mind of Christ" (NIV). You have been given access to God's thoughts. When you come to a situation where despair or anxiety, depression or discouragement would try to steal your hope, you know what to do. You renew your mind by asking God again to exchange your thoughts and view of your circumstances with His. This daily battle is one you can win because Jesus has already secured the victory for you. Rather than fight to win, you fight to stand on the ground that Jesus has already gained.

Dad, even the strongest men need to rest in what Jesus accomplished on their behalf. You are a man of great faith. You know what Jesus has done for you. You know how to take every thought and require it to submit. You are a dad who knows the power of having the mind of Christ.

LET'S PRAY

Lord, this dad spends much of his time in his thoughts. He has planned for his family's future in his mind. He has sought wisdom and made decisions with the mind You've given him. Yet sometimes his thoughts race and he feels afraid, or discouraged, or even depressed. Help this dad renew his thoughts today. If he needs additional support, help him find the right counselors or doctors to bring him peace and hope. He is confident of the victory You secured on his behalf. Help him stand in that today. In Jesus' name we pray. Amen.

CONTINUE THE CONNECTION

Take time this week to pray about the battle in your mind. What is the Lord directing you to do next?

80

TONIGHT WE PRAY FOR THE DAD WHO FEELS AS THOUGH NOTHING IS AS IT SHOULD BE

The gospel of John relates a story of Jesus sharing a meal with His disciples. It was a preparation for the feast of Passover, and since Jesus was the host of the proceeding, the disciples were looking to Him to fulfill all the appropriate religious ceremonies. But there was much anxiety this night because nothing was as it should have been. Jesus had begun by asking them if He could wash their feet, a seemingly inappropriate ceremony. There had been a strange dispute among them involving Judas when Jesus had ordered him away from the table. Jesus told Peter that before the day was complete, he would deny who Jesus was. Jesus also told Thomas that Jesus would be leaving to prepare heavenly residences for all of them, but that after three years together, none of them was strong enough to come with Him. This yearly Passover feast was far from what they had experienced in the past.

Thankfully, one of the disciples asked how they would ever manage without Jesus to teach them. What did this meal tonight represent?

Jesus then told all of them that they would carry on just as they had been. They would complete their tasks, and everything would become clear. He reminded them first that they loved each other and they would come together as a family. And He said in John 14:27, "Peace I leave with you. My peace I give to you. I do not give to you as the world gives. Your heart must not be troubled or fearful." Because of this peace, they never needed to be afraid. It would all be okay.

We must trust that what was true for these men is true for us and our families. Even if what we are experiencing doesn't make sense, the God who loves us is the One who has been teaching us and preparing the steps ahead for us and who will go with us as everything unfolds. It might seem as though nothing is as it should be, but it is all very clear to God.

LET'S PRAY

Lord, even when life seems uncertain, it is clear to You. In the past, this dad has trusted You and has met every challenge as it came. So, Lord, give him rest in the preparation and confidence that he will be successful tomorrow no matter what unfolds. Give him vision to see what You see for him and for his family. In Jesus' name we pray. Amen.

CONTINUE THE CONNECTION

Take time this week to ask the Lord to fill you with the peace He promises.

81

TONIGHT WE PRAY FOR THE DAD WHO KNOWS THAT EVERY TALENT GIVEN TO HIM IS IMPORTANT

*W*hen we think of the apostle Paul, we might think about his ministry to various churches, the letters he wrote that make up a good portion of our Bible, or the ways in which he expanded the gospel of Jesus. What you might not remember is that Paul was a tentmaker. Acts 18:2–3 says, "Paul went to see them, and because he was a tentmaker as they were, he stayed and worked with them" (NIV). The next verse says, "Every Sabbath he reasoned in the synagogue, trying to persuade Jews and Greeks." The apostle Paul, a high-ranking member of the religious community, did not hesitate to use the work of his hands to support himself. He might be best known for his spiritual work, but he saw the physical work he did as important as well. This is because he knew that every talent given to him came from God.

Paul often spoke about talents and giftings. In his first letter to the Corinthians, he said, "There are different kinds of gifts, but the same

Spirit distributes them. There are different kinds of service, but the same Lord. There are different kinds of working, but in all of them and in everyone it is the same God at work" (12:4–6 NIV).

Remember, you have unique talents, and God values all of them because He is at work in all of them. Isn't that what we really want? To know that God doesn't just care about what we consider the spiritual parts of our lives but will use every part of our lives for His purposes? Because if God cares about it, then that means He is helping us with it. And if He cares about what we set our hands or minds to accomplish, we can trust Paul's words are true. There are different kinds of working, but in all of them the same God is at work.

LET'S PRAY

Lord, this dad has accepted the responsibility from day one to do everything necessary to take care of his family. He uses all his talents and gifts to provide what they need and to work for Your kingdom. Strengthen his resolve to see everything he sets his mind and hand to as important. In Jesus' name we pray. Amen.

CONTINUE THE CONNECTION

As you go through your week, remember that the talents and gifts God has given you will benefit your family and connect you to other believers. They are all for a purpose.

8 2

TONIGHT WE PRAY FOR THE DAD
WHO PLANS FOR THE FUTURE

*A*s we go through our days, we are creating the future that God has for us. By that I mean everything we do today affects tomorrow. Our actions carry eternal effects. This is why we pay attention to what we make of our time and our talents.

There is a parable in Matthew 25:14–15 about planning financially for the future that sheds quite a bit of light on this topic. Jesus told a story, saying, "Again, it will be like a man going on a journey, who called his servants and entrusted his wealth to them. To one he gave five bags of gold, to another two bags, and to another one bag, each according to his ability. Then he went on his journey" (NIV). Each servant received value according to their previous successes, and each one was expected to utilize their skills and abilities and prepare for the future when the ruler would return. Later, when he did return, each servant presented the ruler with more than the original investment, except one servant. Unfortunately, that servant returned with nothing except the original asset, having done nothing to improve the investment or prepare for the ruler's return. The wealthy ruler blessed each productive steward and made him a ruler in his own right, with the assets each had produced from the initial investment. The man who produced nothing gained nothing.

The Lord used this parable to teach us to prepare wisely for tomorrow, not just financially but in all areas of our lives. We invest in our family today, knowing it will influence tomorrow. We invest in our marriages, knowing it will affect tomorrow. We invest in the assignments the Lord has given us, remembering that they will be what we build on tomorrow. Make no mistake. God is already contemplating what you will be doing tomorrow and what sort of success you can have with the wise use of today's reward.

LET'S PRAY

Lord, just like the servants who were blessed, this dad doesn't expect anyone else to fulfill his responsibilities. He does his utmost to fulfill Your plans. You have expectations for him, and he plans ahead to complete them. Continue to bless him as he prepares for his future and the future of his family. In Jesus' name we pray. Amen.

CONTINUE THE CONNECTION

Ask the Lord to show you how you can prepare for the future and make even better use of your gifts and talents.

83

TONIGHT WE PRAY FOR THE DAD WHO IS MISSING HIS CHILDREN

*I*n today's world, for so many reasons, dads and their children are sometimes separated by time and space. Work responsibilities can keep them apart for weeks or months at a time. Attorneys and judges can make decisions that require families to be divided. Grown children often make lives in faraway places. The dedicated dad can struggle to maintain connection. That expectation, that desire, that love never goes away.

Jesus explained this love of a father in what we call "the parable of the prodigal son," but it could just as easily be called "the story of a father and his family." Luke 15:11–32 begins the story:

A certain man had two sons. And the younger of them said to his father, "Father, give me the portion of goods that falls to me." So he divided to them his livelihood. And not many days after, the younger son gathered all together, journeyed to a far country, and there wasted his possessions with prodigal living. (NKJV)

There are many details in this story, but at the end, there is reconciliation and joy. What the younger son "wasted" was restored out of the goodness of the father's heart.

While it is easy to see this parable describing our own relationship with our heavenly Father, it certainly relates to our earthly and natural desire to bring our children close in every way possible. Regardless of why there might be distance between you and those you love, remember this: because God is faithful to care for us in our absence from Him, we can know that our children are also never out of our reach. Our faithful prayers continually cover them wherever they are.

LET'S PRAY

Lord, this dad wants his children to know that as long as he has plenty, they will never have lack. Whether it is his time, attention, or finances, he doesn't consider their age or station. Regardless of their circumstances, this dedicated dad looks to see how he might help. This dad is missing his children. Bring his family closer to each other and to You. In Jesus' name we pray. Amen.

CONTINUE THE CONNECTION

This week, pray for each of your children by name. Think of those who may feel out of reach and ask the Lord to bring you closer.

84

TONIGHT WE PRAY FOR THE DAD WHO WANTS TO BE THE VERY BEST

*T*here can be a great deal of satisfaction in being the very best at something. Our own accomplishments take many forms, of course. Many of us have competed for a prize—a job, a raise, or a marathon, perhaps. In all these endeavors, eventually a winner was declared, the most qualified earned the promotion, or the most proficient person became "the best." In life we often experience measuring and judging and eventually a title of some sort. When it comes to your identity as a son of God, "best" is determined by an entirely different standard.

Paul the apostle, no stranger to competition, had an understanding of Greek society and knew there was no greater accomplishment than to beat an opponent on a field of endeavor. People remember winners, Paul often wrote in so many words. But he also wrote in his letter to the Philippians, "I focus on this one thing: Forgetting the past and looking forward to what lies ahead, I press on to reach the end of the race and receive the heavenly prize for which God, through Christ Jesus, is calling us" (3:13–14 NLT). Paul was clearly reminding his readers that God does not judge His children as if they were in competition with one another. *Best* is not determined by lining up all the other competitors and measuring them against one another. Rather, each person runs their own race toward their own mark.

Dad, you are always pressing forward. You know that you can't rest on yesterday's accomplishments. Your high calling is always in front of you. That is how you become your personal best. You press on and become a little better than you were yesterday. You become a little closer to Jesus.

LET'S PRAY

Lord, this dad is determined to complete his journey. Give him fresh spiritual eyes so he can see the road in front of him and dedicate tomorrow to You. He knows that Jesus sets the standard that he gets to follow. He isn't trying to earn his position as a son; he's simply trying to be the best son and the best reflection of Your Son he can be. Give him strength for his race. In Jesus' name we pray. Amen.

CONTINUE THE CONNECTION

As you pray this week, bring forward the areas in your life in which you are striving for excellence. The Lord is very interested in everything you do.

85

TONIGHT WE PRAY FOR THE DAD WHO WISHES HE COULD CHANGE SOMETHING ABOUT HIMSELF

$\mathcal{D}$ad, have you ever wished you had a particular characteristic that would make people know you in a more positive way? Or maybe you wish that you didn't have some perceived character flaw that sets you back in peoples' eyes.

Luke 19:1–3 tells a story about a man who was short and how Jesus interacted with him. "He [Jesus] entered Jericho and was passing through. There was a man named Zacchaeus who was a chief tax collector, and he was rich. He was trying to see who Jesus was, but he was not able because of the crowd, since he was a short man." Tax collectors were truly despised in Jesus' society. They were shunned in polite company. So for this man to even attempt to mingle in the crowd, or attempt to push through the crush of people, took great courage on his part. The scripture does not say that Zacchaeus wanted to know "where" Jesus was but, rather, "who" Jesus was. Zacchaeus realized that

Jesus was the "who" who could change Zacchaeus's life. And he knew that if Jesus saw him, Jesus could change him. The story continues that Zacchaeus climbed a tree, and Jesus saw and acknowledged him and told him that they would dine together at Zacchaeus's house that very day.

Dad, Jesus knows all about your character; He knows all about your flaws, He knows about all your disabilities; perceived as well as real. In the story, when Zacchaeus climbed that tree, he was saying to the people that no matter what he did for a living, he was just as much a person as they were. Jesus sees you just as He sees all His children. And He wants you to have that same confidence in Him. Listen: if you want Jesus to change your life, He can and He will. He already sees you, and He is proud of your daily courage.

LET'S PRAY

Lord, this dad loves You with all his heart. He knows that he is the dad You provided for this family. And he wants You to change him to be more like You every day. Give him the confidence to go forward, and just as you did with Zacchaeus, dine with him today. In Jesus' name we pray. Amen.

CONTINUE THE CONNECTION

Jesus sees and knows you personally. What do you want to say to Him today? What are you hoping He helps you become?

86

TONIGHT WE PRAY FOR THE DAD WHO DOESN'T LIVE A DOUBLE STANDARD

*Y*ou know the importance of making sure others can trust your word. Your nos mean no and your yesses mean yes. When you say you're going to consider something that is asked of you, you will put in the effort to make sure your advice is sound and your help is pure. You do this because you know that in everything you do, you represent God.

Scripture relates a story using the example of just and true weights. God declared in Deuteronomy 25:13–15,

> You must not have two different weights in your bag, one heavy and one light. You must not have two differing dry measures in your house, a larger and a smaller. You must have a full and honest weight, a full and honest dry measure, so that you may live long in the land the Lord your God is giving you.

Throughout the Law and the books of the prophets (written before Jesus walked the earth), unequal or uneven weights were considered an abomination. Why? Because in a sense, just weights represented the truth of the law of God as well as the judgment of God. There was only one way, and there continues to be only one way, to measure.

What does this have to do with us? Dad, you don't have a double-standard life. You have one standard that you follow, and that is Jesus. As you use His standards to measure every part of your life, you set Him as the standard for your family. You are a just and honest man, and in that, you represent Jesus well.

LET'S PRAY

Lord, this dad makes sure he deals fairly in all things. His reputation is valuable, and he trades on it. He knows that others can count on him, and he is a good judge of character. He knows when others are dealing unscrupulously, and he calls them out in order to save others' business opportunities, relationships, and livelihoods. The more he reflects Your character, the more You bless him with opportunities to represent You well. Open his eyes to see Your road of virtue in his daily life. In Jesus' name we pray. Amen.

CONTINUE THE CONNECTION

This week, consider how you represent Jesus in everything you do.

87

TONIGHT WE PRAY FOR THE DAD WHO NEEDS DIRECTION

*S*o, Dad, you have found yourself at a crossroads in your life. You've been traveling a path for some time now. You've seen the scenery, and you know what to expect, but suddenly you come to an unexpected fork in the road. It's time to make a choice in which way to go. You want to make the best choice you can with the knowledge you have.

So I have a question for you, Dad: Have you asked for guidance from your heavenly Father? Scripture tells us to go straight to God. Hebrews 4:16 says, "Let us therefore come boldly unto the throne of grace, that we may obtain mercy, and find grace to help in time of need" (KJV). We can come to God with everything we need, in every aspect of our lives. At the end of the day, it's all about prayer. The best part about asking God which way to go is that He knows all the paths; He knows about all the pitfalls and all the opportunities that are available to us when we ask.

Scripture tells us in James 1:17 that God gives us every good and perfect gift. His guidance is always good guidance. He will give us exactly what we seek. Even if you don't know what to ask for, or where to go, God does, and He wants what's best for you. Jesus talked about this when He said, in Matthew 7:9, "What man among you, if his son asks him for bread, will give him a stone?" Here's the point: we have permission to approach our heavenly Father for wisdom, and when we ask for it, He won't trick us with bad advice. He always gives the real thing. We can trust that His heart is kind and His answers are good. If you need direction, you don't have to figure it out on your own.

LET'S PRAY

Lord, this dad needs answers about which direction to go. A path is set before him, and he wants to make the best decision. So we come before You to ask that You make the way plain. Help him hear You clearly. Give him perfect guidance that each step will be the right one in the right order to the right destination. In Jesus' name we pray. Amen.

CONTINUE THE CONNECTION

Pause to consider the roads in front of you, and listen for your heavenly Father's voice. He wants to lead you.

88

TONIGHT WE PRAY FOR THE DAD WHO HAS STRENGTH OF CHARACTER

*A*nyone can say they will trust God and follow Him when times get hard and the pressure is on. But it takes a strength of character to live this out when the moment comes.

Three men named Shadrach, Meshach, and Abednego remind us through their story the importance of remaining true to what we believe, and the goodness of God to show up when we do. In the book of Daniel, we learn these three men had seats in King Nebuchadnezzar's government. There had been a decree issued that required all to bow and worship a gold statue the king had erected. When the king found out these men would not bow, Nebuchadnezzar threatened to throw them into a furnace, questioning who would save them from his power. They replied: "Nebuchadnezzar, we don't need to give you an answer to this question. If the God we serve exists, then He can rescue us from the furnace of blazing fire, and He can rescue us from the power of you, the king" (3:16–17).

The three men spoke boldly in confronting the king.

Nebuchadnezzar questioned whether the God of Shadrach, Meshach, and Abednego even existed. Our three heroes responded in kind. "We don't even have to think about our answer to you. And you won't have to wonder who that God is very long, because He will rescue us from the fire and then He will rescue us from you." You likely know the ending. Three men were tossed into the fire, but a fourth man walked with them in that fire, and the men survived. The God they served proved Himself real and faithful. He will do the same for you.

LET'S PRAY

Lord, we pray for the dad who believes in his own strength of character. He does what he does because it's the right thing to do. And he is always prepared for the challenges that arise, just like Shadrach, Meshach, and Abednego were. This dad is dedicated to his family and determined to live for You because he has received so much. Remind him that his character is an accurate representation of You. You are real, and You are real in him. In Jesus' name we pray. Amen.

CONTINUE THE CONNECTION

We all go through trials. What fiery furnace is threatening to consume you, and what characteristic helps you remember that God will protect you?

89

TONIGHT WE PRAY FOR THE DAD
WHO GOES FOR THE GOAL

*S*ome people participate in ultramarathon races, Ironman competitions, and high-endurance trials with the sole purpose of finishing the race. Maybe you've done this—subjected your body, your mind, and certainly your will to a grueling competition that might take not just minutes or hours but possibly days.

These competitions require immense preparation, but mostly they require a determination to begin and a dedication to finish. Any dad who enters these races knows that the hardships involved will be immense. They know that they may not finish first, but finishing is the goal.

Hebrews 12:1 says, "Since we also have such a large cloud of witnesses surrounding us, let us lay aside every weight and the sin that so easily ensnares us. Let us run with endurance the race that lies before us."

In the race that Paul described, just like in the races of today, most of the glory was found in the finishing. There may have been a crown in Paul's day, or a wreath, but years after the end of the competition, no one but those who competed know what was truly achieved. Only those who have competed before will understand what the hardships were, what was endured, and what was gained. These competitors will carry the pride of finishing within themselves.

Dad, you take the challenges that come as they come every day. Not because of a crown but because the Lord said that you can do this. And your competition is for the rest of your life. It is forever. This race has always been about endurance. That is the goal for you. To endure and then to finish. Dad, at the end of the day, you and the Lord know what you've achieved.

LET'S PRAY

Lord, this dad knows that he has a race to run forever. He prepares every day for the challenges that lie ahead in taking care of his family. And he takes all the necessary steps because he is dedicated to them and determined to carry them to wherever You may lead them. Remind this dad of his victories, that he might have confidence in future blessings. In Jesus' name we pray. Amen.

CONTINUE THE CONNECTION

How can you go for the goal today?

90

TONIGHT WE PRAY FOR THE DAD WHO IS ENVIOUS OF WHAT SOMEONE ELSE HAS

*T*he tenth commandment of the Lord speaks to us of wanting what is not already ours. Exodus 20:17 says, "You shall not covet your neighbor's house. You shall not covet your neighbor's wife, or his male or female servant, his ox or donkey, or anything that belongs to your neighbor" (NIV). All the coveted things referenced in this commandment are things that fulfill the neighbor's life. God would not have us wish for or desire our neighbor's life.

First of all, God knows that if we want what someone else has strongly enough, our desires can overtake our souls. And secondly, when we decide that what our neighbor has is more valuable than what we have, we are, in effect, telling God that we are not satisfied with what He has already provided. Finally, when God tells us not to do something, He always has a plan for us instead. Here, where He says not to be reaching for things that belong to others and what we think might make us happy or fulfilled, His alternative is for us to reach for Him and know an even greater peace than what those things can provide.

Dad, it can be so easy to watch the neighbor pull into their driveway with the new car, see the online photo the friend shared of his family on vacation, or even listen to your own relative share about their big Christmas bonus and wonder, *Why not me?* But Scripture reminds us that when we are busy envying, we leave little room for thanksgiving.

LET'S PRAY

Lord, this dad may have a desire to have more stuff, and that's getting in the way of his happiness. It's hard not to desire new, different, or exciting things and to think that's the key to happiness. However, You give us everything we need for our good. Help this dad see the value of what he already has and to see Your goodness. Show him the path to gratitude. In Jesus' name we pray. Amen.

CONTINUE THE CONNECTION

Take a moment to make a mental list of all the blessings in your life. Pause to thank God for each one.

91

TONIGHT WE PRAY FOR THE DAD WHO TEACHES HIS FAMILY TO HONOR THE LORD

*O*ne of the best things we can teach our children is to honor and revere God. In Scripture we read about Abraham, who had a son named Isaac. Remember, Abraham (then Abram) had been called to leave his homeland and follow God. God had promised Abraham that he would be a father to many nations, and Abraham believed God. So when God told him to gather all of the implements of a sacrificial offering and to take his son (who represented the seed of many nations) up to a mountain to sacrifice him, Abraham obeyed.

As Abraham took his willing son up the mountain, he turned to the men traveling with him and said, "Stay here with the donkey. The boy and I will go over there to worship; then we'll come back to you" (Genesis 22:5). Abraham fully believed the promise that God was going to make him a great nation, but he was also willing to fully honor God, holding nothing, even his beloved son, back.

As Abraham was about to sacrifice Isaac, God called out to Abraham again. "'Do not lay a hand on the boy or do anything to him.

For now I know that you fear God, since you have not withheld your only son from Me.' Abraham looked up and saw a ram caught in the thicket by its horns. So Abraham went and took the ram and offered it as a burnt offering in place of his son. And Abraham named that place The Lord Will Provide" (vv. 12–14).

Just as Abraham loved Isaac more than his own life, as a dad your whole life is about your love for your family. You are always looking toward the fulfillment of God's promise. You prepare your family for the journey you will take together like it's all you will ever do. You're taking all of them with you, and they will always have enough because, like Abraham, you know the Lord will provide. It's in this walk of faith as a family that we teach the greatest lesson. God is who He says He is, so we will honor Him.

LET'S PRAY

Lord, just like Abraham, there are many mountains for this dad to scale. He has continually determined to seek You and to teach his family to honor and revere You. Help him live with peace in the journey and with maximum focus and maximum effort for his family. Remind him to lean into You as he raises his family to trust You. In Jesus' name we pray. Amen.

CONTINUE THE CONNECTION

Take a moment to remember what God has specifically called you and your family to do for Him. In each obedient act, you honored Him with your yes.

92

TONIGHT WE PRAY FOR THE DAD WHO UNDERSTANDS DIVINE ECONOMY

$\mathcal{J}$ohn 6:11–12 records another story of Jesus feeding a multitude. He was given a few loaves of bread and fish,

> And Jesus took the loaves; and when he had given thanks, he distributed to the disciples, and the disciples to them that were set down; and likewise of the fishes as much as they would. When they were filled, he said unto his disciples, Gather up the fragments that remain, that nothing be lost. (KJV)

Jesus performed many miracles during His ministry. He knew that His heavenly Father had provided the loaves and the fish, and Jesus thanked Him for the blessing. Many of the people were blessed with the provision. And what remained didn't go to the ground. It was gathered.

In this, Jesus taught His disciples a valuable lesson. He taught them about blessings to come that would be so great that the circumstances couldn't contain them. He showed them that miracles aren't just for the people there; they are for the people who will be affected by them later.

Dad, you need to understand that in the divine economy, there is always more than enough. And whatever miracle has occurred in your life will touch others in a way you can't fathom. When you go about your day, living as you do in the miracle-working power of Jesus, you will encounter others who need the power you have. Luke 6:38 reminds us to "give, and it shall be given unto you; good measure, pressed down, and shaken together, and running over" (KJV). Miracles are never just for us. In God's economy there is enough of what Jesus creates to bless everyone.

LET'S PRAY

Lord, this dad lives in the miracle of Your salvation. He knows that everything he has has come from You. As he goes about his daily tasks today, he asks that You multiply the blessings in his life, so that there would be more than enough for today, with baskets left over for tomorrow. And just as Jesus did, he gives thanks to You for his daily bread. In Jesus' name we pray. Amen.

CONTINUE THE CONNECTION

What is something God has supernaturally multiplied in your life? How did you use that to be a blessing to others?

93

TONIGHT WE PRAY FOR THE
DAD WHO SEEKS JUSTICE

*A*s a man who values justice, you notice when there is unfairness or corruption in the world around you. You want to set right what is wrong. This is the heart of your heavenly Father too. Scripture reminds us in Psalm 7:11 that God is a righteous judge. So, I ask you, are you praying about the injustice around you?

Jesus told a parable about prayer, concerning how we should always pray and not faint, especially when it comes to justice. Luke 18:6–8 recounts, "The Lord said, 'Listen to what the unjust judge says. Will not God grant justice to His elect who cry out to Him day and night? Will He delay to help them? I tell you that He will swiftly grant them justice. Nevertheless, when the Son of Man comes, will He find that faith on earth?'" He used the example of a widow who had been treated unjustly by a man in a business dealing. Ordinarily a woman of lesser means, like a widow, would not be engaging in such a matter. In any case, the widow asked the judge to make one of two possible judgments: either even the score between the two families or punish the man by throwing him into prison. Any judge would know these options. Jesus was then clear that justice should be meted out quickly. And God will always hear and respond to the cries for justice from His children.

God has His heart tuned to the cries for justice. He's listening for you to pray and bring the unfairnesses of the world to Him. The key for you, Dad, is to pray that His justice comes quickly, because His wisdom and His response are always better than anything we could come up with on our own.

LET'S PRAY

Lord, this dad seeks justice wherever he goes. He believes that everyone should have the same opportunity and be treated fairly, no matter what station in life they hold. You have said that You will fight for this dad and with this dad to achieve justice in the world. Show him the path for true righteousness for others as he uses Your name to defeat injustices. In Jesus' name we pray. Amen.

CONTINUE THE CONNECTION

If an injustice in the world breaks your heart, you can be certain it breaks God's heart as well. What injustices are you bringing to Him in prayer?

94

TONIGHT WE PRAY FOR THE DAD WHO KNOWS WHAT TO DO

$\mathcal{D}$ads who know what to do when times get tough can carry a heavy burden. We can experience pressure in such circumstances of crisis when all eyes are on us for directions about what to do, but I bet in these situations you step up to the plate and say, "If it has to be, it's up to me." If so, you're with good company.

Matthew 27:57–60 records a story of just such a man named Joseph of Arimathea. After the death of Jesus, it was time to decide what would happen to His physical body and to prepare it for burial. Scripture says, "When it was evening, a rich man from Arimathea named Joseph came, who himself had also become a disciple of Jesus. He approached Pilate and asked for Jesus' body. Then Pilate ordered that it be released. So Joseph took the body, wrapped it in clean, fine linen, and placed it in his new tomb, which he had cut into the rock. He left after rolling a great stone against the entrance of the tomb."

Joseph was a member of the ruling council of Jerusalem. He had to hide his relationship with Jesus because he would have been under a great deal of scrutiny, especially when the council was trying to decide how to deal with Jesus. Joseph had not agreed with much of what the council thought or said about Jesus, or certainly their plans concerning how they might oppose Him. But as a councilor, he knew all the rules requiring the proper burial of a religious person. While these tasks were usually handled by women, he himself carried out this responsibility.

Like Joseph, there are times when it would be so much easier to let someone else handle it. But as a dad who knows what to do when times get tough, you don't pass the buck. You care about making sure what should be done is done. And it matters.

LET'S PRAY

Lord, You have given this dad wisdom to know what to do and how to take care of his family and perhaps friends and those in his community. He is the dad who knows what to do and how to step up to make that happen. He is who he is because he wants to be. The responsibility is heavy, but he knows that in Christ he is strong enough to accomplish every goal. Give him the confidence to decide and the courage to step forward. In Jesus' name we pray. Amen.

CONTINUE THE CONNECTION

The next time someone needs your help, remember that everything you do for others you do for the Lord as well.

95

TONIGHT WE PRAY FOR THE DAD WHO MUST RELOCATE HIS FAMILY

The nativity story includes the visit of three wise men, bringing gifts of gold, frankincense, and myrrh to Jesus and His family. While we picture these men present shortly after His birth, we know that some time had actually passed before they arrived with these offerings. Scripture says in Matthew 2:13, "After they were gone, an angel of the Lord suddenly appeared to Joseph in a dream, saying, 'Get up! Take the child and His mother, flee to Egypt, and stay there until I tell you. For Herod is about to search for the child to destroy Him.'"

King Herod had learned from the wise men who studied the prophecies that a child had been born who would be King of the Jews. King Herod also understood the danger of a soon-to-be king in his midst and gathered his scribes to study their own records to see when such an event might take place. Herod's reputation preceded him, and the people of Bethlehem worried about the possibility of political unrest, especially once they discovered that a King had come to reside with them.

So God supernaturally directed Joseph to flee with his family out of the Roman Empire and certainly out of the reach of this particular governor. This fulfilled an Old Testament prophecy that the life of the Messiah would be protected. Do you know how Joseph was able to safely relocate his family and fund this expensive journey? They had everything they needed with the wise men's generous offerings.

God is aware of your circumstances, Dad, and no matter what He calls you into next, know that He has already prepared you to protect and care for your family.

LET'S PRAY

Lord, this dad knows there are uncertain times now and ahead. He always looks out for his family's safety in all their circumstances. Sometimes the peace of a particular home or environment has to be uprooted because of job opportunities or perhaps for the care of a loved one living far away. It's disruptive to everyone, especially the children, who must reorient their lives with little or no experience in such a change or upheaval. You have this dad's peace prepared just for him. Make Your voice as clear as it was to Joseph and Mary. In Jesus' name we pray. Amen.

CONTINUE THE CONNECTION

Whether you're planning a relocation or a change in some other area of your life, how do you sense God preparing you now?

96

TONIGHT WE PRAY FOR THE DAD WHO KNOWS JESUS IS THE PRIZE

*I*f you were to ask a friend who didn't know Jesus what his goal was in life, his answer would likely differ widely from yours. He might say wealth, or status, or security. Sure, you'd like all those things as well, but you don't aim for them. You aim for Jesus, knowing that when you give Him everything you have, you get Him and every good gift He has for you.

Jesus told a story about the kingdom of heaven, where the economy and the attitudes are different from the worldview most of us live in. In Matthew 13:45–46, He said, "The kingdom of heaven is like a merchant in search of fine pearls. When he found one priceless pearl, he went and sold everything he had, and bought it."

Jesus knew all about merchants, as Nazareth, where Jesus grew up, was near a well-traveled trading route. The merchant described by Matthew looked only for the prize of fine pearls. He would make trips far and wide to buy pearls. He would know the value of his journey, and he would know the value of his purchase. And there would be no amount too large to pay for one particular pearl. He would determine that the pearl was worth any price, and he would sell everything he had to own it, if necessary.

You, Dad, are that merchant. Nothing stands in the way of your relationship with the Lord. You know where He can be found. You don't wait for someone to tell you where to look. You actually enjoy the journey because you remember the joy of finding Him in the past in unexpected places and seasons. He's worth it. He is the prize. And when you find Him, you feel like you've won. Because you have.

LET'S PRAY

Lord, this dad dedicates himself to excellence. He's always sought after You, and his children watch and learn. They expect their dad to continually follow Christ, because that is who he is. This dad trains them up in the way they should go, and the tree of their lives grows straight (Proverbs 22:6). You've blessed this dad abundantly. Help him stay on the right path. In Jesus' name we pray. Amen.

CONTINUE THE CONNECTION

This week as you pray, remember how anything that must be given to gain a life in the presence of God is always worth it.

97

TONIGHT WE PRAY FOR THE DAD WHO FACES CHALLENGES IN PARENTING

*B*eing a dad isn't easy. Challenges come. We overcome them only after much time, work, perhaps money, and, of course, prayer. But because they often come without warning, and usually without regard to other life circumstances, it's easy to feel overwhelmed. It's easy for all of us to wonder if there is ever going to be a break in the seemingly never-ending stream of daily trials.

Yes, you have prepared to do the things that keep your kids safe and sound. And the fact that you are still standing means that you've overcome a challenge or two already. As a matter of fact, in life there tends to be a certain repetition, and you will probably see these same struggles again. But in that repetition you will see what has worked in the past and what will likely work again. It is the strength that you've always found in Christ. Because of that, you don't quit. Why? Because every day you choose this life. And that means you keep working through its challenges, including the challenges that come with parenthood.

Psalm 127:3–4 says, "Children are a gift from the LORD; they are a reward from him. Children born to a young man are like arrows in a warrior's hands" (NLT). In this, the psalmist reminds us there is no greater blessing than the promise of children in a family. Like arrows, we must learn how to guide them, but God assures us that when we give our greatest attention to our children, He will bless all other work of our hands.

LET'S PRAY

Lord, this dad meets the challenges of raising children head-on. It doesn't come easy, and there is no to-do list that works for everything. But this dad is equipped to work through every challenge, no matter how big or small, because You're on his side. Comfort him to know that even when he feels overwhelmed with the responsibilities of raising children, his children are a gift from You. Give him the assurance he needs to address tomorrow with courage and confidence. In Jesus' name we pray. Amen.

CONTINUE THE CONNECTION

This week as you pray, take your challenges before the Lord, remembering that He is not the author of trials but the giver of solutions and answers.

98

TONIGHT WE PRAY FOR THE DAD WHO HAS MADE IT THROUGH ANOTHER DAY

*H*ow are you doing today, Dad? You got it done and have the bruises to show for it. You're pretty sure you could have done better if the day had been just a little longer. But, still, the house is standing, and the doors are locked. You've taken care of what needed to be done. You've prayed for each member of the family.

And for many of us, that's not just making it; that's prospering. You know you have to keep going, Dad. Even when the challenges seem too tough, the troubles multiply, and your energy is depleted. Sometimes the fact that you keep going is a testament to your faithfulness.

The apostle John wrote a letter from his place of exile, the Isle of Patmos, after he'd been sent there by the Roman emperor Domitian. He said, "Dear friend, I pray that you may prosper in every way and be in good health physically just as you are spiritually" (3 John v. 2). When you're in exile, there are few rewards and few blessings. So in his own quiet way, John took care of those in need. John encouraged his friend and prayed that he might prosper in all areas of his life, mentally, emotionally, and physically, even as it is clear that his work for the Lord has prospered him spiritually.

Dad, the Lord knows your life and your dedication. You're not in exile like John, but you're a recipient of the encouragement he offers. And as you go from day to day, you will have the same prosperity in your spirit that will carry over to your whole life. Keep going, Dad.

LET'S PRAY

Lord, today this dad loved his family the best way he knew how. When he rose in the morning, he thought about what was best for his children and set about doing it. He knew what his family needed and wanted. So he kept going today, completing the tasks to get them all to tomorrow. And he knows that You have a plan that will bless all of them. Smile on this dad who is making it, and reward him with another day of blessing. In Jesus' name we pray. Amen.

CONTINUE THE CONNECTION

This week, as you think of all that God has done for you, pause to be encouraged. You are a dad who keeps going, because you know who your strength is.

99

TONIGHT WE PRAY FOR THE DAD WHO IS GRATEFUL FOR HIS FAMILY

*J*ames 1:17 reminds us, "Every good and perfect gift is from above, coming down from the Father of the heavenly lights, who does not change like shifting shadows" (NIV). You've been given good gifts. Some might sit on shelves in your office or hang in your garage. You have special things that your children have wrapped and put under the tree made with love from craft supplies or clay. Maybe you have a treasured item, something of great value that you use sparingly or display proudly. But, Dad, your greatest gift, the one that shows just how much you are loved by your own Father in heaven, is the gift of your family. And you are grateful.

You have been given this gift to nurture and protect. It's a solemn responsibility to be a father, and you have taken it on yourself gladly because you recognize the importance and value of what God has given you in this sacred trust. Your family is who you wake up in the morning thinking about and who you go to sleep at night praying for. You stand between them and the world, because they are precious to you. There is surely no greater gift.

God chose just the right dad to care for this family He loves. He knew you would love them as He does, protect them as He does, and provide for them in every way you can. So every day you get up and do just that. You are determined to show God and your family that they can trust you. And you are grateful for the trust God already has in you.

LET'S PRAY

Lord, this dad knows the value of what he has been given. His family sees his commitment to them and how much he wants to take care of them. He knows that the responsibilities are lifelong, but he was chosen for this task and given the opportunity to succeed. He is grateful. Bless him tonight. In Jesus' name we pray. Amen.

CONTINUE THE CONNECTION

Pause tonight to consider each member of your family and think of something about them that you are grateful for.

100

TONIGHT WE PRAY FOR THE DAD
WHO REMEMBERS HIS STORY

A staff, or a rod, is spoken of often in Scripture, but I wonder if you know that the staff wasn't just a stick—it was a story. On a man's staff, he would carve reminders of important moments in his life. For example, David, as he protected his father's sheep, likely had carved a reminder of when he had killed a bear or when he had killed a lion. Men remembered what God had done for them and kept a history of it.

Dad, you might not carry a staff, but you do keep records in your heart. You know that God has been faithful and will remain faithful. So even on the days that don't go as planned—maybe something comes up at work or maybe one of the kids gets sick and you're just the dad to fix it—you know God is with you.

The psalmist wrote in Psalm 23:4, "Even when I go through the darkest valley, I fear no danger, for You are with me; Your rod and Your staff—they comfort me."

As King David spoke these words, he likely remembered that he had a rod of God in his hand. This rod had carved on it the exploits and the successes David had experienced and where God had protected David from both expected and unexpected trials. The rod was always with David. Because a traveler would use the rod as he walked, it would always be in front of him. And he would see God's promises of safety every single step he took. David was saying, "No matter what I face, I don't have to be afraid, because You're protecting me just like I protected the sheep—and I have my own rod of record to prove it."

When changes arise, we often fear that we are not prepared for what lies before us, but God is assuring you that most of the time, when you review your history, and see God's rod in your hands, this challenge isn't all that new after all (Psalm 23:4).

LET'S PRAY

Lord, this dad knows that he can do what You've called him to do, and he tries to always be prepared. But sometimes changes cause him to doubt his preparation. He's risen to the occasion before, but this task looks different. Remind him to think back over his successes and what he has overcome in the past to help him move forward. In Jesus' name we pray. Amen.

CONTINUE THE CONNECTION

What is carved on your staff? Take a moment to remember God's faithfulness to you and let it bring you comfort.

CONCLUSION

Before you go . . .

*Y*ou did it, Dad. You finished the book. (Or maybe you're like me and like to skip to the end of what you're reading to see if you get something special for finishing the book. You know, some word of wisdom that can change your life, not just for the better, but for the best.)

Here is that word of wisdom before you go: this book was written just for you, but there was likely one devotion that was an "aha" moment for you. There was one that you *know* was written specifically for you. Read it again. Know the scripture within it like you know your own name. Hear the voice of God say, "I see you, Dad, and I'm with you." Hear Him say, "No matter what you might think, I love you like a Father loves a son, and you are not alone." Listen when He says, "I will never leave you to your own devices if you call on Me." And then . . . start at the beginning of the book again. Read about your heavenly Father's love for you, what it means to have a dad and to be a spiritual dad for your children. Then read the prayer for a hopeful dad, or the dad who needs a new outlook, or the dad who counts on God. See yourself once again as God sees you, warrior that you are, fighting in the trenches for your family against all odds, overcoming every trial that comes your way.

And keep going, Dad, because you've got this.

ABOUT THE AUTHORS

BECKY THOMPSON is a bestselling author and the creator of the Midnight Mom Devotional community, gathering over one million moms in nightly prayer. Speaking hope into the struggle of balancing life as a wife, mother, and daughter of God, Becky has become the voice of modern Christian motherhood. You can learn more about Becky's top Christian podcast, *Revived Motherhood*, or find more of her work by visiting BeckyThompson.com. Becky lives near Nashville with her husband, Jared, and their three children.

DR. MARK R. PITTS is a graduate of the University of Tulsa Law School. He is an ordained pastor and a well-known Bible teacher in the Oklahoma City, Oklahoma, area where he lives with his wife, Susan. They have been married for forty-one years and have two adult daughters and three grandchildren. In 2019, Mark created the Midnight Dad Devotional online community with his daughter, Becky Thompson, the creator of the Midnight Mom Devotional. Mark enjoys teaching Scripture and praying for dads just like you.

JOIN THE NIGHTLY
GLOBAL PRAYER MOVEMENT
with Mommas Just Like You

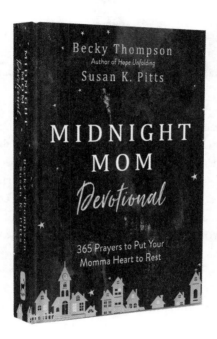

The end of the day can bring so many
feelings to the surface of a momma's heart.
Pray alongside a community of women
who feel just like you do.

Author Becky Thompson and her parents, Dr. Mark and Susan Pitts, are the founders of the Midnight Mom and Midnight Dad Devotional online prayer communities. They lead more than 1.5 million parents worldwide. With prayers, devotions, online courses, and more, as a parent you will find strength for your journey. You will realize that no matter what time of night or day, your heavenly Father travels with you. The Midnight Mom and Midnight Dad Devotional ministries equip you to tackle both the hard and joyful places on this journey of being a parent. Join the global prayer movement with others just like you.

www.midnightmomdevotional.com

beckythompson.com/midnight-dad-devotional/